Diversity, Equity and Inclusion in Honors Education

Diversity, Equity and Inclusion in Honors Education

Edited by

Graeme Harper

Cambridge
Scholars
Publishing

Diversity, Equity and Inclusion in Honors Education

Edited by Graeme Harper

This book first published 2018

Cambridge Scholars Publishing

Lady Stephenson Library, Newcastle upon Tyne, NE6 2PA, UK

British Library Cataloguing in Publication Data
A catalogue record for this book is available from the British Library

ISBN (10): 1-5275-0636-3
ISBN (13): 978-1-5275-0636-7

CONTENTS

DIVERSITY, EQUITY AND INCLUSION IN HONORS EDUCATION: AN INTRODUCTION

GRAEME HARPER

The Organization for Economic Co-Operation and Development notes the following in its 2008 policy brief *Ten Steps to Equity in Education*:

> Equity in education has two dimensions. The first is *fairness*, which basically means making sure that personal and social circumstances – for example gender, socio-economic status or ethnic origin – should not be an obstacle to achieving educational potential. The second is *inclusion*, in other words ensuring a basic minimum standard of education for all – for example that everyone should be able to read, write and do simple arithmetic. The two dimensions are closely intertwined. . . . [1]

Fairness and inclusion: by the OECD definition here, the former is perhaps more obvious to those involved in honors education and the latter perhaps less obvious, given that honors education focuses upon, and has long focused upon educational achievement more so than access to education. Yet, the OECD definition unequivocally states "the two dimensions are closely intertwined". Intertwined, not merely related. Thus, attention to the pursuit of fairness is also attention to the pursuit of inclusion, and vice versa.

How then can honors education – and in the case of the discussions in this book, largely honors in higher education – support the intertwined deals of fairness and inclusion? And if it does not do so, how can it claim to be offering principled "opportunities for measurably broader, deeper, and more complex learning-centered and learner-directed

---

[1] OECD, *Ten Steps to Equity in Education,* http://www.oecd.org/education/school/39989494.pdf (2008), 2.

experiences for its students"?[2] Further still, by direct reference to the notion of "being included" inclusion references the ideal of diversity, and equity, by its reference to "impartiality" clearly suggests freedom from bias. Are these things therefore not fundamental to an honorable honors education?

Ten Steps to Equity in Education goes on to discuss the design of education and resources needed, and is ultimately much more of a brief concerned with elementary and secondary education than with post-secondary education. But the suggestions made in it are nevertheless a productive starting point for a discussion of diversity, equity and inclusion in college honors education. Not least because *Ten Steps to Equity in Education* says this:

> Traditionally, education systems have sorted students according to attainment. Evidence from studies of secondary and primary schools suggests that such sorting can increase inequalities and inequities . . . [3]

This surely must prompt us to ask if we in college honors education, for all our promotion of community service and support for aspiration and recognition of commitment and touting of the foundational importance of a civic responsibility, are in fact contributing to societal inequity rather than challenging it. Even the possibility of that surely cannot be acceptable.

The majority of the chapters in this book began as presentations at the first annual conference of the National Society for Minorities in Honors (NSFMIH), held at Oakland University, Michigan in March 2016. The NSFMIH (www.nsfmih.org) was founded the year before that, in an effort to bring together and further advance discussions, and action, in relation to diversity, equity and inclusion in honors education. Annual NSMIFH conferences have been held since then. Some of the chapter writers here, while not attending that first national NSFMIH conference, responded energetically to a 2016 call for additional explorations and lively contributions.

---

[2] National Collegiate Honors Council, Definition of Honors Education, https://www.nchchonors.org/uploaded/NCHC_FILES/PDFs/Definition-of-Honors-Education.pdf (2013)
[3] OECD, *Ten Steps to Equity in Education,* http://www.oecd.org/education/school/39989494.pdf, 3.

In **Chapter One**, Simon Stacey and Jodi Kelber-Kaye explore inclusive excellence at the University of Maryland, Baltimore County (UMBC), an institution well-known for its contribution to inclusive education and one whose long-time president, Dr. Freeman Hrabowski III, has made a notable personal contribution to improving diversity and educational equity in US higher education. Chapter Two offers an examination of "bringing together studies of great texts and intergroup dialogue". Trisha Posey, Director of the Honors Scholars Program at John Brown University, "a comprehensive Christian liberal arts university located in Northwest Arkansas" inspiringly concludes that "it is clear that incorporating intergroup dialogue into the student class experience had immediate and long-lasting impacts on students in the area of cross-cultural engagement."

In **Chapter Three**, Laura Hanna moves the conversation into the realm of professional advising, relating work going on in Valdosta State University's Honors College in Valdosta, Georgia. One of her most interesting discoveries is related in the section "Group Advising as a Bridge for Achieving Creativity and Inclusion", where she notes that a "more collaborative technique diffuses the authority to allow students to learn about the sorts of projects they can complete from their peers who actually completed the projects". Perhaps indeed we sometimes forget that general student empowerment can aid inclusivity in honors, even provide a hub around which it can revolve. **Chapter Four** sees this book's editor consider the philosophy and ideal of Ubuntu, and its application to honors education.

Marty Dupuis, Vanessa McRae and Zholey Martinez, writing of their experiences in The Burnett Honors College at the University of Central Florida, discuss "a pilot mentoring program" called The Elevation Fellows Program "established through a partnership between The Burnett Honors College and Elevation Financial Group" in **Chapter Five**. They analyze "the donor relationship with the community partner supporting the work of college access for underserved, economically disadvantaged high school students". This is followed by Rod Raehsler's exploration of minority student recruitment in honors programs at rural colleges and university in **Chapter Six**. Raehsler very usefully suggests some possible solutions.

In the wonderfully collaborative **Chapter Seven**, Peter Bradley, Jordan Dawkins, Melanie Trinh, Cindy Tran and Caitlyn Toering offer a case study of the 20 year old Honors Program at Ferris State University and a project to "make recommendations about how [the program could] better appeal to minority students". While in **Chapter Eight**, Matt Jordan offers "a criterion for determining which sorts of views, if any, may be considered out-of-bounds in an honors community", strongly concluding that "our best approach is one that mandates respect for each individual as well as open inquiry concerning every topic compatible with that respect".

In the final two chapters of the book, we move from California State University, Fullerton, with Sandra Pérez's "Understanding Diversity in Honors at a Large, Public, Comprehensive, Hispanic and Pacific Islander Serving University" in **Chapter Nine** to Purdue University in **Chapter Ten** with Dwaine Jengelley and Jason Ware's tiered mentorship study: "Multi-Year Initiatives For Enhancing Diverse Students' Outcomes Within Large Public Honors Colleges and Programs" – an excellent concluding chapter due to its emphasis on the merits of "structured intentional interaction". In other words, a positive, productive approach to diversity, equity and inclusion in honors education does not come about only through discussion but through intentional action.

It is recognized that *Diversity, Equity and Inclusion in Honors Education* is not on its own conclusive or even comprehensive. Its editor and its contributors would never suggest otherwise. It is hoped, however, that this is a book that contributes to raising of awareness of the possibilities of diversity, equity and inclusion in honors education, that it offers some practical indications of how this might be approached, and that it encourages others to take action.

CHAPTER ONE

INCLUSIVE EXCELLENCE IN HONORS EDUCATION AT THE UNIVERSITY OF MARYLAND, BALTIMORE COUNTY

SIMON STACEY AND JODI KELBER-KAYE

Introduction

This chapter describes how the Honors College at the University of Maryland, Baltimore County (UMBC) diversified its student membership. UMBC is well-known for its commitment to inclusive excellence, but until fairly recently, the Honors College, which ought to be a prominent site of inclusive excellence, did not fully make good on that commitment.[1] The initiatives employed over the past five years to make the Honors College inclusively excellent include:

- intensive, highly focused and multi-channel recruiting and/or outreach, to both applicants and potential applicants to the Honors College;
- a growing mentoring partnership with an anchor high school in Baltimore City, the urban area nearest to UMBC;

---

[1] The UMBC Honors College is not unique in facing diversity challenges. Honors Colleges and Programs at non-HBCUs rarely enroll substantial numbers of Underrepresented Minority (URM) students. See, for example, R.R. Harrison-Cook, *An Examination of Issues Affecting African American Students' Decisions to Enroll in Honors Programs or Honors Colleges at Predominantly White Postsecondary Institutions*, Unpublished Doctoral Dissertation, University of South Carolina, Columbia, 1999. Harrison-Cook's convenience sample found that African American students made up between 1.1% and 6.7% of the population of the Honors Colleges and Programs surveyed, with most clustered around the lower end of the range. (pp. 3-4)

- an admissions process revised to be more holistic, flexible and sensitive to the many forms that academic promise can assume.

Though these initiatives are still being developed and refined, the demographic profile of the incoming freshman Honors College classes at UMBC has changed markedly over the past five years. In what follows we describe the impetus for our inclusive excellence effort, the different initiatives that made it up, aspects of what we believe helped make them successful, and where there remains room for improvement.

Background: UMBC and its Honors College

Established in 1966, UMBC is a medium-sized public research extensive and doctoral degree granting university emphasizing excellent undergraduate programs in the liberal arts and sciences and engineering. UMBC's undergraduate academic programs include 48 major degree programs, 38 minor programs, and 25 certificate programs. UMBC combines the emphasis on teaching found at liberal arts colleges with the innovation of a research university. The Carnegie Foundation ranks UMBC in the category of Research Universities with "Higher research activity."

UMBC's 2016 freshman class of 1,538 students was among the most diverse in the nation (45% minority, including 24% Asian, 14% African American, and 7% Hispanic and Native American). The class was also academically capable. It included dozens of high school valedictorians, students with 4.0 GPAs, and students with highly competitive SAT scores (a 1216 average SAT for top quartile students), and the average high school GPA of the class is 3.75. There is no stable achievement gap in the six-year graduation rate between white and African American freshman students (though a gap remains for white vs African American male transfer students).[2] UMBC's undergraduate population numbered 11,142 in 2016, and approximately 60% of all undergraduates enroll with an interest in STEM.

The Honors College at UMBC was established in 1988, and developed from an existing Honors Program. It enrolled its first class of eighty-one students in the Fall of 1989. The Honors College curriculum has evolved ever since, but currently requires that students take Honors Forum in their first semester at UMBC (freshmen only), complete six

---

[2] UMBC Institutional Research, Analysis and Decision Support, *Retention and Graduation Rates*, http://oir.umbc.edu/university-data/retention-graduate-rates/.

appropriately distributed Honors classes, an Applied Learning Experience and a writing course. Honors classes take the form of Honors Sections (enhanced versions of existing classes) and Honors Seminars, which are stand alone, small-group, discussion-focused classes taught by Faculty Fellows selected through a competitive application process.

In the close to thirty years of its existence, the Honors College has awarded approximately 1500 Certificates of Honors to UMBC graduates, and its graduates have gone on to prestigious graduate and professional schools in the U.S. and abroad, winning national and international awards such as the Goldwater Scholarship, the Marshall Fellowship and Gates Cambridge Fellowship, Fulbright Scholarships, and others. The average GPA of our graduates is above 3.7, and in recent years most Valedictorians and Salutatorians have been members of the Honors College. The membership of the Honors College is kept small (currently about 500 students, less than 5% of the total undergraduate population) in order to provide the personal quality of attention that is supposed to be the hallmark of Honors education.

The origin of the focus on inclusive excellence, and a path not taken

In retrospect, several factors coincided to jumpstart the UMBC Honors College's inclusive excellence effort. The first was the visit to Honors Forum of the university's President. Honors Forum is a mandatory class, designed to introduce first-year students to each other, the Honors College, and UMBC. One major feature of the class is that faculty and staff from around the campus are invited to visit the class and speak about their work or research, to help provide the students with a sense of the variety of activities taking place on campus. Perhaps the most anticipated visit is that of Dr. Freeman Hrabowski III, the university's charismatic President. After his 2011 visit to the class, Dr. Hrabowski noted to the Dean and Vice Provost of Undergraduate Education, to whom the Honors College reports, that the Freshman Honors College class was not nearly as diverse as the rest of the campus, and urged that efforts be made to remedy this problem. Dr. Hrabowski was not mistaken in his observation. In that year, the 82-person freshman class included only one underrepresented minority (URM) student. Nor had he observed something anomalous. The Honors College was indeed generally, and not just in this freshman class, less diverse than the campus around it.

That year also saw the appointment of an Honors College Associate Director well equipped to attend to this deficit. She had a longstanding commitment to diversity and inclusion, a record of encouraging it as a faculty member in the Gender and Women's Studies Department at UMBC and in her ongoing research, and extensive connections to Baltimore City (and its public schools), a majority African American city less than ten miles from UMBC.

The high-level injunction to pay more attention to diversity, and the simultaneous appointment of an Associate Director with the right mix of skills and commitments, made 2011 the right time to design a plan to diversify the Honors College, while maintaining its rigorous standards. This was not the very first time the lack of diversity in the Honors College had attracted attention. But in prior years, a rather desultory diversity plan had focused on "double-dipping" into the university's flagship inclusive excellence program, the Meyerhoff Scholars Program (MSP). The MSP is a national model for efforts to increase diversity in the STEM fields and while it is open to students of all backgrounds, these students must demonstrate a commitment to advancing underrepresented minorities in these fields.[3] The MSP typically enrolls a majority URM student class each year, and these students had seemed like a ready-made population from which to recruit diverse students for the Honors College. But the MSP has a very well-defined mission, which requires students focus intently on preparation for a STEM PhD program. There was some understandable apprehension that the demands of the Honors College curriculum might divert MSP students from that focus. Furthermore, the MSP is explicitly dedicated to supporting STEM students, and the UMBC Honors College, like almost all Honors Colleges, seeks a disciplinarily balanced mix of students. At a university and Honors College with a majority STEM student population, relying extensively on recruiting Honors College students from the MSP risked increasing demographic diversity at the expense of diminished disciplinary diversity. Accordingly, while the MSP would play a role in the Honors College's diversity effort, the bulk of our energy went in different directions.

---

[3] For more on the Meyerhoff Program, see Kenneth I. Maton, Shauna A. Pollard, Tatiana V. McDougal Weise, and Freeman A. Hrabowski III, "The Meyerhoff Scholars Program: A Strengths-based, Institution-wide Approach to Increasing Diversity in Science, Technology, Engineering and Mathematics," *Mt. Sinai Journal of Medicine* 79(5), September 2012, pp. 610-23.

Working with what we already had: Mining our existing applicant pool, and the university's

The Honors College receives as many as 3500 applications in some years, for an entering freshman class we hope will number around 100. The members of the small application reading team, inevitably, must make some hard decisions about where to focus their file-reading energy, and one way to rationalize the process is to focus on the applications from students who appear, numerically, to be the strongest--those with the highest GPAs and SAT or ACT scores. But these quantitative measures do not always pick out all of the most capable and promising students, and we know that we miss some truly excellent students simply because their abilities are not well-captured by their grades and test scores. Though this issue remains a hotly contested one, there is persuasive evidence that URM students, and especially African American students, are disadvantaged by standardized tests.[4] One of our first 2012 initiatives was therefore to identify URM applicants who, while admissible to the Honors College, might not ordinarily have had their applications read early in the process, and to examine their application files. Doing so allowed us to gauge--from the record of accomplishments not captured in the numerical data, from the quality of writing, from the story of opportunities seized and obstacles overcome--which of these otherwise potentially overlooked students merited further consideration.

A second step was to try to ensure that all of the URM students who had applied to UMBC were apprised of the opportunity that the Honors College represented. We were concerned that some highly capable URM students might simply not have been aware of the existence of the Honors College and its advantages, or might have ruled themselves out and not applied. To address this problem, we obtained from the Office of Admissions and Enrollment Management the names and contact details of high-performing URM (and other) UMBC applicants who had not applied

---

[4] An early contribution to this debate was R. Freedle, "Correcting the SAT's Ethnic and Social-Class Bias: A Method for Re-estimating SAT Scores," *Harvard Educational Review*, 2003 73(1), 1–44. Freedle's work was questioned on methodological grounds, but his original findings have since been confirmed (see M. V. Santalices and M. Wilson, "Unfair Treatment? The Case of Freedle, the SAT, and the Standardization Approach to Differential Item Functioning," *Harvard Educational Review 2010,* 80(1), 106-133.) The ACT appears to replicate the bias of the SAT. (see R. Reeves and D. Halikias, "Race Gaps in SAT Scores Highlight Inequality and Hinder Upward Mobility," *Brookings Papers on Social Mobility*, February 2017.)

to the Honors College. An intensive outreach campaign was then organized for these students. It entailed reading their UMBC application essays and materials, and then using Honors College stationery to hand write notes to them, mentioning aspects of their history, trajectory or aspirations that suggested they would find the Honors College a congenial and rewarding place, and inviting them to call, e-mail or visit (a staff member's business card was always included in the mailed correspondence). In its first years, the writing of notes (well over a hundred each spring) was undertaken by the Director of the Honors College. In subsequent years, other members of staff joined the process, both to spread the burden, and so that note-writers could, where possible, write to students with backgrounds or interests similar to their own. Though we did not know this at the time, and our outreach was directed at a variety of students, this note-writing approach followed one of Harrison-Cook's recommendations: to provide "information [that] will help African American students understand what honors education involves, what honors education requires of them, and how honors education can benefit them."[5]

Third, the Honors College reached out not only to students qualified to apply to the Honors College in the hope of turning them into actual applicants, but also to students who had been admitted to the Honors College but whom we had not yet yielded. The goal here was to explain from their perspectives what the advantages of Honors College membership were. While this effort targeted many of our admitted students, we were careful to ensure that URM students were included. In its most recent iterations, the campaign has also included notes from sophomore Honors College students, who spend a pizza and soda-fueled evening with Honors College staff writing them. The rationale for the inclusion of students was that some of them had received notes as they were deciding which offers of admission to accept, and might remember which parts of the message resonated with them, and that some applicants might respond better to a communication from students just barely older than them. (At any rate, it was certainly true that notes from students had a flavor and an energy all their own, often including cartoons and sketches, poetry, anecdotes and other unique approaches to connecting with applicants.)

Finally, after May 1--National College Decision Day--the Honors College reached out again to students (URM and others) who had accepted their UMBC offer of admission and who had been admitted to the Honors

---

[5] Harrison-Cook, *An Examination of Issues Affecting African American Students' Decisions to Enroll*, p. 95.

College, but had not accepted their offer of admission to the Honors College. These students were e-mailed, and invited to discuss the advantages of the Honors College with Honors College staff members.

This suite of efforts made an immediate difference, as the table below demonstrates:[6]

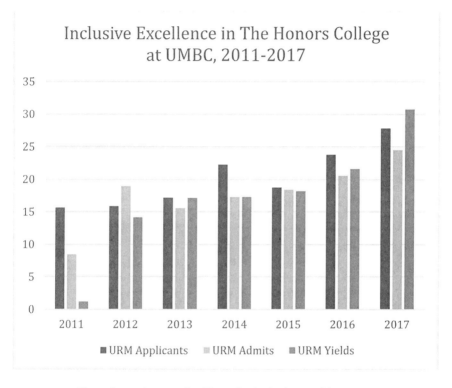

The enhanced outreach efforts also had other positive consequences, too. For instance, take just the first year of the initiative, the 2012 freshman class was more than 25% bigger than the 2011 freshman class, though it is true that the 2011 class was an unusually small one. And, the average SAT score of the freshman entering class increased from 2121 in 2011 to 2144 in 2012.

---

[6] We are very grateful to Alexandra Graves and Michael Stone, the Honors College's Academic Advisors, for valuable assistance in collecting, cleaning and analyzing the data represented in this table.

Making more of what we need: Rethinking recruitment in Baltimore City

The approach described above clearly produced some encouraging results. The UMBC Honors College in 2017 is a much more diverse place than it was in 2011, and that change has brought with it all the well-documented advantages and benefits one would expect.[7] But in a sense it remained the case that the Honors College was simply maximizing opportunities it could (and should) always have been exploiting. As the momentum generated by our refinements to our admission and recruitment processes grew, we began to look for other ways to foster the Honors College's inclusive excellence.

UMBC has long cherished a variety of strong connections to Baltimore City, and the Honors College shared some of these connections. Until budgetary constraints ended it, the Honors College orientation involved a City-as-Text excursion every year, and the mandatory freshman service-learning experience often takes place at sites in the city. But the Honors College had not adequately incorporated Baltimore--and especially the Baltimore City Public School System (City Schools)--into its recruitment planning and practice.

Recruiting from City Schools would serve the cause of inclusive excellence in two ways. First of all, Baltimore City's, and its public school-going population, is predominantly URM: 80.6% of the public school population is African-American, and 9.4% is Hispanic or Latino.[8] So, increasing the number of students from Baltimore City who matriculate to UMBC and join the Honors College would likely have a positive effect on the Honors College's ethnic and racial diversity. Second, much of the population City Schools serve is of relatively low socio-economic status: 64.7% of City Schools students are classified as "low income,"[9] higher than for any other school system in Maryland, and a rate

---

[7] For perhaps the canonical statement on this issue, see W. G. Bowen and D. Bok, *The Shape of the River: Long-Term Consequences of Considering Race in College and University Admissions* (Princeton, NJ: Princeton University Press, 2000).

[8] Baltimore City Public Schools, *City Schools at a Glance*, http://www.baltimorecityschools.org/about/by_the_numbers, accessed July 26 2017.

[9] Baltimore City Public Schools, *City Schools at a Glance*, http://www.baltimorecityschools.org/about/by_the_numbers, accessed July 26 2017. The low income designation is "based on eligibility for programs including Medicaid, Temporary Assistance for Needy Families, and Supplemental Nutrition Assistance."

which compares unfavorably with the national average.[10] So, recruiting from City Schools would enhance the socio-economic diversity of the Honors College as well.

In addition, UMBC as a whole has not recruited City Schools students at what might be regarded as an appropriate rate. In recent years, the total number of students attending UMBC who graduated from City Schools ranged from a low of 31 to a high of 57, with an average of 40.5. So, the Honors College's turn to the city was welcomed by many of the stakeholders on the UMBC campus (especially in the Office of Admissions and Enrollment Management), who recognized that a City Schools student recruited to the Honors College who would not otherwise have been was, a student recruited to UMBC who might otherwise not have been.

Our most recent effort, then, focuses on Baltimore Polytechnic Institute (colloquially known as Poly), one of the highest-performing public high schools in Baltimore City, and considered to be the STEM magnet high school in the city. After Poly's application to offer the College Board's AP Capstone class was approved, the course was offered for the first time in the 2015-16 academic year. AP Capstone is a "program that equips students with the independent research, collaborative teamwork, and communication skills that are increasingly valued by colleges." The course is "comprised of two AP courses: AP Seminar [for Juniors] and AP Research [for Seniors]- and … [p]articipating schools can use the AP Capstone program to provide unique research opportunities for current AP students."[11] The two teachers primarily responsible for the implementation of AP Capstone were committed to providing these unique research opportunities, and looked to UMBC and the Honors College to help provide research mentorship and expertise for their students.

Serendipitously, one of these two teachers was a UMBC graduate and, to boot, the spouse of an Academic Advisor in the Honors College. This represented a golden opportunity for the Honors College to strengthen the cordial but mostly coincidental relationship it had until then had with Poly, and to build the fabled "pipeline" from high school to college. Discussions with the Poly AP Capstone staff resulted in a plan to pair UMBC faculty and staff mentors with Capstone students to help supervise their research projects. The mentorship relationship was to entail

---

[10] In 2013, low-income students constituted the majority of students in the United States for the first time. Southern Education Foundation, *A New Majority: Low Income Students Now a Majority In the Nation's Public Schools* (January, 2015).

[11] College Board, *AP Capstone Overview*, https://advancesinap.collegeboard.org/ap-capstone.

multiple in-person meetings each semester between mentor and mentee, visits to campus by students for an introduction to the library and other academic resources on campus, to the process of research, and--our ulterior motive--to college life, to UMBC and to the Honors College.

The inaugural AP Capstone class graduated in June of 2017. At the urging of their mentors, and the Honors College staff, 14 of the 18 students applied to UMBC. In years past, the number of Poly students applying to UMBC has ranged from 59 to 87 with an average of 76. Applications to UMBC from Poly (the entire school) for Fall 2017, as of this writing, jumped to 102. We cannot, of course, be sure that students in the AP Capstone mentored by UMBC faculty and staff class would not have applied anyway, but the increase in the number of applicants to UMBC from Poly for Fall 2017 admissions is at least suggestive. On the other hand, the yield of AP Capstone students was not what might have been hoped for. Only one student decided to attend UMBC, though she did also (thankfully!) become a member of the Honors College.

Though disappointing, this outcome was not entirely unexpected. It would certainly have been gratifying to see more Poly AP Capstone students matriculate to UMBC and join the Honors College in the first year, but it is really the long-term payoff that we hope will justify the effort. For instance, one of our current challenges is that as we talked to the first eighteen Poly AP Capstone students about the advantages of the Honors College, we had only one member of the Honors College *from Poly* to help make that case for us. We can now add one more student voice at least to the chorus singing UMBC's praises, and that student will have a strong connection to the AP Capstone experience. Also, we anticipate that the greater visibility of UMBC and the Honors College at Poly, and the solidification of the relationship between our two institutions, will tend to increase the number of students who have UMBC 'on their radar,' with the result that even some students who are not part of the AP Capstone program will begin to consider it, and the Honors College, as destinations.

Finally, many City Schools students need significant non-loan financial aid in order to attend college. To address this need, we established (with assistance from the Office of Admissions and Enrollment Management) a set of Memorandums of Understanding between the Honors College and UMBC's specialty scholars programs,[12] and City Schools. This arrangement allows the Honors College and each scholars program to provide a four-year annual merit scholarship to at least one

---

[12] "Scholars Programs at UMBC,"
http://undergraduate.umbc.edu/apply/scholars.php.

student graduating from a Baltimore City public high school. UMBC's seven named scholars programs--the Center for Women in Information Technology Scholars, the Cyber Scholars, Meyerhoff Scholars, Humanities Scholars, Linehan Artist Scholars, Sherman Teacher Education Scholars and Sondheim Public Affairs Scholars--are competitive, scholarship-granting programs intended for students with particular academic interests. They "combine financial awards with special opportunities for advanced research, unique seminars, directed internships, study abroad and more." Cross-membership of the Honors College and a scholars program is heartily encouraged, and commonly taken advantage of. The funding arrangement was launched in Fall 2016 and the Honors College was able to provide significant scholarship funding to one student in Fall 2016 and another (the AP Capstone student, in fact) in Fall 2017.

What have we learned?

As is true of everything that happens in higher education, the job is never done (or, as our university President likes to say, 'success is never final.') Our inclusive excellence effort will continue, and continue to be refined, for the foreseeable future. But, summarized below are some of the lessons we've learned in the past five years, and which will continue to guide us in the future:

Take advantage of a propitious moment or set of circumstances. Our inclusive excellence effort was galvanized by the coincidence of a directive from the President and the arrival of a staff member equipped to carry it out. The collaboration with Poly was facilitated by the personal connections between Poly and UMBC staff. Honors Colleges have many priorities (diversity just one amongst them), and sometimes have to choose between them. But when the planets align to support the pursuit of a particular objective, it makes sense to seize the opportunity.

It helps to align your own efforts with university priorities. The Honors College and the university both aspired to establish and improve relationships with Baltimore City schools. The meshing of these interests allowed the Honors College to make (limited) claims on university resources to support this work that it otherwise might not have been able to make.

Increasing diversity happens one student at a time. Sometimes, an organization or institution can rely on its reputation and stated mission to attract diverse students. The highly successful and nationally-recognized MSP is an example. The Honors College, on the other hand, has to sell itself energetically to diverse students, one at a time. We hope at some point to achieve critical-mass, a happy situation in which we can rely on the twinned fact and perception of our diversity to perpetuate and solidify our inclusive excellence. But for us, for now, increasing diversity is a person-by-person effort, and this is probably true for most Honors Colleges.

It may not be clear what worked. We are confident that our efforts played a causal role in increasing the diversity of the Honors College, but we have not been able to disaggregate the effects of particular initiatives. For instance, we cannot say whether outreach to high-performing non-applicants to the Honors College, or extra attention to already admitted students, 'paid off' best. We find ourselves in a position a little bit like businessman John Wanamaker, who allegedly once said: "Half the money I spend on advertising is wasted; the trouble is I don't know which half." In the same way, we know at least some of our efforts have paid off in greater diversity in the Honors College; we just don't know which ones!

The job is not done when the entering freshman class is more diverse. Diversifying an entering class is obviously the essential first step. But it is, arguably, more important still to support the members of a newly diversified class all the way to graduation, and beyond. The benefits of having been an Honors College member even for a short period may be significant, but they pale into comparison to graduating with an Honors College certificate, and we owe it to these students (as we do to all students) to ensure they enjoy those benefits.

CHAPTER TWO

"DIFFERENT CULTURES CAUSE ME TO HESITATE": INTRODUCING INTERGROUP DIALOGUE IN AN HONORS GREAT TEXTS COURSE

TRISHA POSEY

Introduction

Incorporating experiences of cross-cultural engagement into existing curriculum can be a challenge. Nevertheless, experiences in dialogue across difference are essential if honors students are going to be effective leaders in civil society, the workplace, and their families. For these reasons, the Honors Scholars Program at John Brown University adopted as an imperative the revision of the HSP curriculum to include education in cross-cultural engagement. One of the first classes to undergo curricular revision was the Honors Western Civilization course, two sections of which are offered in the spring semester each year. While there were limits to the effectiveness of the curricular revisions, the incorporation of intergroup dialogue into the course proved to be an effective means of developing the cultural competency of JBU honors students.

Background—John Brown University and Diversity

John Brown University is a comprehensive Christian liberal arts university located in Northwest Arkansas. It is a largely residential college with a traditional undergraduate population of 1300. The university is situated in Siloam Springs, a town of 15,000 located near the Oklahoma border. The undergraduate student population is largely drawn from students in Arkansas, Oklahoma, Texas, Missouri, Colorado, and Kansas. Most students (79%) identify as Caucasian. The African-American student population is quite small (2%), and the non-US citizen student population is at 7%.[1] However, a number of the Caucasian students come from missionary families and grew up overseas, so that about 15% of the student population consists of students who spent their formative years outside of the United States.[2]

Institutional surveys of students reveal that John Brown University struggles in the area of providing cross-cultural experiences for our students. The JBU data from the Coordinated Institutional Research Project (CIRP) consistently show that students show little development in "Pluralistic Orientation" compared to students in the JBU comparison group.[3] For the 2011 First-Year CIRP assessment, 43% of JBU students were identified as having low pluralistic orientation, compared with the 30.2% of students at comparison institutions.[4] While the same cohort of students scored higher in the area of Pluralistic Orientation their senior year (46.8% self-identified as competent in this area), they still fell behind students at peer institutions (50.2% of whom self-identified as competent in this area).[5] Institutional numbers from the National Survey of Student Engagement are even more concerning. The 2014 NSSE survey of JBU students revealed that first-year students were more likely to engage in discussions with diverse others than were their senior-level peers.[6] Sadly,

---

[1] "JBU Facts 2016-17," John Brown University, accessed December 1, 2016, http://www.jbu.edu/about/facts/.

[2] "Missionary Kids," John Brown University, accessed December 1, 2016, http://www.jbu.edu/admissions/international/mks/.

[3] Pluralistic Orientation is defined as "Ability to work cooperatively with diverse people, tolerance of others with different beliefs, openness to having my own views challenged, ability to discuss and negotiate controversial issues, and ability to see the world from someone else's perspective." This information comes from the John Brown University Office of Institutional Effectiveness, "2011 CIRP Freshman Survey, CIRP Construct Reports, First-time, Full-time Freshmen, John Brown University," accessed December 1, 2016, https://eaglenet.jbu.edu/resources/oie/Assessment%20Data/Coordinated%20Institu tional%20Research%20Project%20(CIRP)/Freshman%20Survey%20(TFS)/2011/ TFS_2011_PDF_CONSTRUCT.pdf.

[4] Ibid.

[5] John Brown University Office of Institutional Effectiveness, "2013-2014 Diverse Learning Environments Survey," accessed December 1, 2016, https://eaglenet.jbu.edu/resources/oie/Assessment%20Data/Coordinated%20Institu tional%20Research%20Project%20(CIRP)/Diverse%20Learning%20Environment s%20(DLE)/2014/0091_-11-DLE_2014_XLS_FACTORS.pdf.

[6] John Brown University Office of Institutional Effectiveness, "NSSE14 Engagement Indicators," accessed December 1, 2016,

NSSE numbers in the Honors Scholars Program were even worse. Students in the Honors Scholars Program scored lower in the area of "Discussions with Diverse Others" compared to their non-honors peers (with the exception of students of "Other Economic Backgrounds" for first-year honors students), and they also saw a decrease in cross-cultural engagement over their time at JBU (with the exception of engaging with students of "Other Political Views," which went up slightly).[7]

These results are inconsistent with one of the explicitly stated learning outcomes for the JBU Honors Scholars Program, which is to "understand one's culture, as well as appreciate and learn from people of differing backgrounds and beliefs as acts of Christian hospitality." In order to address the need for opportunities for cross-cultural engagement in the JBU Honors Scholars Program, in the spring of 2016 the HSP joined the great texts curriculum for Honors Western Civilization II with experiences in intergroup dialogue.

Great Texts and Intergroup Dialogue

In bringing together studies of great texts and intergroup dialogue, the JBU Honors Scholars Program was joining two things that might seem like strange bedfellows. After all, one of the critiques of great texts programs is that they tend to be Western-centric, focus on texts written by white men, and offer little in the way of diverse perspectives. The great texts approach to education grew out of a movement of American academics in the 1920s and 1930s who were concerned by the increasing specialization of the academy and sought to reclaim the educational ideal of educating for wisdom through the study of great ideas as presented by Western philosophers, theologians, and writers. Books in the great texts canon include texts like Plato's *Republic*, Dante's *Divine Comedy*, and the writings of the American founders. Despite the narrow representation of authors in the great text canon, there is a good deal of overlap between the goals of teaching great texts and those of intergroup dialogue. Great text approaches to teaching focus on reading whole texts for the purpose of developing wisdom. Reading and discussing great texts provides students

---

https://eaglenet.jbu.edu/resources/oie/Assessment%20Data/Forms/Assessment%20 Data.aspx?RootFolder=%2Fresources%2Foie%2FAssessment%20Data%2FNation al%20Survey%20of%20Student%20Engagement%20%28NSSE%29%2F2014&F olderCTID=0x012000DCCD5B402094E6499F4D7A9FD6DEBF94&View=%7B CDFC3F35-C695-4660-BFDB-2237D6306B86%7D

[7] John Brown University Office of Institutional Effectiveness, Report by email, August 29, 2016.

the opportunity to ponder deep questions of human existence: Who am I? What is my purpose? What can I know? How should I live? Many of these questions are also addressed in the intergroup dialogue experience, which uses "a pedagogy that creates learning communities where members share and learn from each other's experiences, reflect on their own and other's experiences to make sense of larger structural systems of advantage and disadvantage, and create new meanings for themselves."[8] The natural overlaps between great text classrooms and intergroup dialogue provide for an effective pedagogical pairing that has the potential to transform students.

Intergroup dialogue is a well-developed pedagogical technique that provides highly structured experiences for students for the purpose of cross-cultural engagement and personal transformation. It grew out of a movement in the early 1990s to foster conversations about conflict and accelerated after President Bill Clinton instituted his "Initiative on Race" in the mid-1990s.[9] Since then, a number of researchers (many of them affiliated with the National Intergroup Dialogue Institute at the University of Michigan) have launched projects and research studies related to intergroup dialogue. Intergroup dialogue brings together students from different groups (usually with a history of conflict) for the purpose of engagement in a facilitated experience.[10] There are four stages to intergroup dialogue[11], including:

> **1. Forming and Building Relationships**. In this stage, the instructor develops an environment in which "honest and meaningful dialogue" can take place.[12] At this point the goal is to help students feel comfortable talking about difficult topics with each other. Part of the discussion centers on laying ground rules for engagement, with an emphasis on respecting others and listening to their experiences.

---

[8] Maurianne Adams et. al., *Teaching for Diversity and Social Justice*, 3rd ed. (New York: Routledge, 2016), 29.

[9] David Schoem et. al., "Intergroup Dialogue: Democracy at Work in Theory and Practice," in *Intergroup Dialogue: Deliberative Democracy in School, College, Community, and Workplace*, eds. David Schoem and Sylvia Hurtado (Ann Arbor: University of Michigan Press, 2001), 1-2.

[10] Ximena Zúñiga et. al., "Intergroup Dialogues: An Educational Model for Cultivating Engagement Across Differences," *Equity and Excellence in Education* 35 no. 1 (2002): 7.

[11] Ibid., 10-12.

[12] Ibid., 10.

2. Exploring Differences and Commonalities of Experience. This stage is meant to provide students with an opportunity to explore their identities in particular groups and then identify ways in which cross-group interactions can create conflict. This stage involves both activities that require self-reflection (such as exploring early memories related to group membership) and activities that bring members of differing groups together.

3. Exploring and Dialoguing about Hot Topics. Moving beyond reflection to fuller engagement, students in this stage are provided an opportunity to discuss topics that are usually considered controversial through a facilitated dialogue experience. In an interracial dialogue, for example, one topic that might be explored is police shootings of unarmed black men. Through the course of the dialogue students are challenged to listen to each other across their differences and to consider how they might shift their understanding of a particular topic, if necessary.

4. Action Planning and Alliance Building. In this fourth and final stage, students are encouraged to develop a plan of action based on their new understandings. Suggestions for change can be both personal and group-oriented.

In the spring of 2016 the Honors Scholars Program at JBU combined readings in great texts with intergroup dialogues in the areas of gender and race and supplemented the dialogues with exercises in speaking up against offensive statements about others. Two sections of the class (a total of thirty-one students) went through the exercises. Most students in the classes knew each other from the honors first-year courses they had taken the previous semester, and about half of the students had been in a class with the instructor the prior semester. The primary text for the intergroup dialogue experience was Adams's and Bell's *Teaching for Diversity and Social Justice*, which combines contextual readings in a variety of subjects with class and group assignments and experiences for use in the classroom.[13]

---

[13] Adams et. al., *Teaching for Diversity and Social Justice*.

The Experience

Before the students participated in intergroup dialogues, they carried out a cultural diversity self-assessment (Appendix A). This provided a baseline by which the Honors Scholars Program could judge transformation over the course of the semester. Students generally scored themselves in the high median range in this assessment, averaging in the high 3's and low 4's on a 5-point Likert scale. After the self-assessment, the course shifted to readings and discussions related to gender. The students read two texts, Milton's *Paradise Lost* and Wollstonecraft's *Vindication of the Rights of Woman*, which usually stir up discussion on gender issues.

John Milton's *Paradise Lost* (1667), while focused more on the rebellious character and actions of Satan, also spends a good deal of time describing the pre- and post-Fall relationship between Adam and Eve. *Paradise Lost* is notorious for its treatment of Eve, whose relationship with God is described as derivative—only possible through her husband, Adam. Milton clearly expresses this unequal relationship in lines 296-299 of book four in *Paradise Lost*:

> Not equal, as their sex not equal seemed:
> For contemplation he and valor formed,
> For softness she and sweet attractive grace;
> He for God only, she for God in him.[14]

Further on, in lines 637-38 of the same book, Eve says to Adam:

> God is thy law, thou mine; to know no more
> Is woman's happiest knowledge and her praise.[15]

Book four of *Paradise Lost* always sparks intense discussion among students about historical and modern gender relationships and the oppression of women, a discussion that continues in our reading of Mary Wolstonecraft's Enlightenment text *A Vindication of the Rights of Woman*.

Strongly rooted in the Enlightenment idea of personal freedom through the use of reason, *A Vindication of the Rights of Woman* (1792) argues that until women are free to use their minds, without imposition from men who would have them serve only as "pretty things" to be admired, both men and women will suffer. Wollstonecraft rails against the

---

[14] John Milton, *Paradise Lost*, ed. David Scott Kastan (1667; Indianapolis: Hackett Publishing Company, 2005), 120.
[15] Ibid., 131.

limitations placed on women: "Taught from their infancy that beauty is woman's sceptre," she states, "the mind shapes itself to the body, and, roaming around its gilt cage, only seeks to adorn its prison."[16] Wollstonecraft calls out Milton for his oppressive views of women. Both of these texts problematized gender for my students, forcing them to consider whether gender differences are innate or simply social constructs, to what extent social expectations of gender lead to the oppression of men and women, and whether gender-based oppression is common today. The discussion of these great texts thus opens the door to conversation for the first intergroup dialogue.

After reading *Paradise Lost* and *A Vindication of the Rights of Woman*, students participated in a gender intergroup dialogue. Outside of class, students responded to the following question prompts:

> Three things you need to know about me are:
>
> When you were a child, what is one message you were taught about relationships between girls and boys?
> > How were you taught this lesson?
>
> When you were a child, what is one lesson you were taught about how males were supposed to relate to each other?
> > How were you taught this lesson?
>
> When you were a child, what is one lesson you were taught about how females were supposed to relate to each other?
> > How were you taught this lesson?

Students brought their answers to these questions to class, and then they sat on the floor in their gendered groups. We made lists on the board of expectations that students identified for their own gender and the opposite gender. After we made the lists, each group (male and female) was then given five minutes to comment on the effects of these expectations on them. Female students listened to male students as they responded, and then male students listened to female students as they responded. Following these five-minute sessions, students were then permitted to respond to each other.

Several themes emerged from the intergroup dialogue, many of which came through in the post-exercise written reflections. As expressed by Wollstonecraft, many young woman articulated frustration at their

---

[16] Mary Wollstonecraft, *A Vindication of the Rights of Woman*, 2nd ed. (1792; Mineola, NY: Dover Publications, 1996), 43.

embodied experience of gender oppression. One young woman wrote, "For a girl you are pressured to have the perfect slim body, and the designer clothing with makeup that took 3 hours to put on perfectly." The concern over gender expectations went both ways, however. Many young women in class realized, some of them for the first time, that men experienced pressure to conform to gender expectations as well. "Listening to the discussion today made me realize that gender stereotypes also put pressure on guys," one student wrote. Many students expressed frustration with the effects of gendered expectations that kept them from flourishing in relationship with those of the opposite gender. "Cross-gender friendships are really hard," one student expressed, "harder than they should be." The most frequent theme in student responses was the realization that experience played a significant role in student ideas and expectations of gender. As one student wrote, "Overall, talking with different people reminded me that not everyone has my background and therefore universalizing my experience is incredibly dangerous and limiting."

Students thus came away with new understandings about gender, which were shaped both by the texts they read for class and the intentional discussion regarding gender that provided opportunities for listening and sharing with each other.

Mid-way through the semester the students went through their second intergroup dialogue experience after they read *Night* by Elie Wiesel. One of the themes of *Night*, as well as Elie Wiesel's 1986 Nobel Peace Prize speech, is the idea of witnessing to injustice in order to combat it. In *Night*, a young Wiesel reflects on the silence that others showed in the face of the Holocaust, refusing to recognize the seemingly unimaginable destruction of European Jews. Years later, Wiesel articulated the need to speak against injustice, famously stating in his Peace Prize speech, "We must always take sides. Neutrality helps the oppressor, never the victim."

After reading *Night* students engaged in an intergroup dialogue in which they discussed the challenge of speaking up in the face of offensive statements about groups of people. For this dialogue, students first started by discussing why they scored themselves so low on the diversity assessment statement "I challenge others when they make racial/ethnic/sexually offensive comments or jokes." Group discussion on this topic revealed a number of reasons for student silence, including a fear of being seen as self-righteous and an inability to offer articulate responses to offensive statements. Once these issues were identified, the class then went through an exercise in which they were introduced to a common way of addressing offensive statements ("Open the Front Door"[17]) and then practiced responding in mock settings in which offensive were made about race, gender, and religion.

This intergroup dialogue was one of the most challenging to carry out in part because most of the students were hesitant to be viewed as offering critique of others, even those who would speak in derogatory terms about other groups. In a Christian culture that emphasizes "niceness" at the expense of confrontation, students have been given few tools for effective engagement in conflict. Other students simply found the idea of confrontation offensive in itself. In a student evaluation for the course, one student wrote:

> If I were to comment on every time some people make such comments then I would lose those friends and my ability to have an influence in this area. I don't mind if someone else thinks they should do that but I don't think I should and I don't like it when my ability to appreciate cultural diversity is judged based off of questions like this.

Despite the challenges in the intergroup dialogue in this area, students did mark themselves higher in the area of speaking up in their post-dialogue self-assessment. The student self-score for challenging others when they make offensive comments went from a 3.1 to a 3.8. This was still, however, on the lower end of the scale compared to their answers in other areas.

Finally, toward the end of the semester students engaged in an intergroup dialogue related to race. This followed a presentation on the history of racism in the United States and readings and discussions of speeches and essays by Martin Luther King, Jr. This proved, by far, to be the most challenging intergroup dialogue, for a variety of reasons. Race is a difficult topic to discuss, but it has been made even more difficult in recent years by the shooting deaths of people of color. In the Honors Western Civilization class, the discussion was even more difficult because so few students of color attend our university or are members of the Honors Scholars Program. All but three students in two sections of the Western Civilization course were students of European descent, making discussions between groups impossible.

---

[17] Kerry Ann Rockquemore, "Allies and Microaggressions," *Inside Higher Education Online*, accessed December 13, 2016, https://www.insidehighered.com/advice/2016/04/13/how-be-ally-someone-experiencing-microaggressions-essay.

Since most of the students were of European origin and, I surmised, had been provided with few opportunities to consider their own bias and privilege, the approach to the third intergroup dialogue was to carry out an exercise and discussion in implicit bias. The set-up for this dialogue included two class periods in which I outlined the history of oppression against African-Americans in the United States. Topics included race-based slavery, the failure of Reconstruction and the institution of Jim Crow, Post-World War II discrimination, including redlining and the denial of voting rights, and the Civil Rights movement. After this foundation was laid, students read a number of speeches and writings by Martin Luther King, Jr., including "The Power of Nonviolence" (1958), "Letter from a Birmingham Jail" (1963) and "I See the Promised Land" (1968). Topics of discussion included the radical nature of nonviolence as a form of protest, the difference between just and unjust laws (which connected students to earlier discussions on John Locke), and the nature of systematic racism. Following these discussions, students took the "Race" implicit bias text at the Harvard Project Implicit website and then reflected in writing on their results for the purpose of discussion in class.

In the class discussion, which was carried out with students sitting in a circle, students expressed a negative reaction to their scores that was stronger than expected. The vast majority of students received a score of "Strong Preference" or "Slight Preference" for European Americans. Among many students there was a deep sense of disappointment in this result. For most of the students, who had experienced a privileged life as European Americans, coming to grips with the reality of their own implicit bias was emotionally challenging. "So it turns out I am a racist," one student wrote disappointingly.

Many students turned their anger at their score toward the assessment itself—stating that the assessment was designed to produce pre-determined results. While much of the class time was supposed to have been spent on processing results, it turned out that a good deal of time needed to be spent establishing the legitimacy of the results in response to student comments such as "This test seemed fabricated to produce results that made the test-taker appear more prejudiced than they may actually be." As another student stated, "In my heart I am not a racist. This cannot be correct."

Despite the initial resistance in class, students were more willing in their written responses to reflect more fully on the meaning of their results. One student freely admitted, "Different cultures cause me to hesitate." Many students also admitted that their life experiences had heavily shaped their assessment results. "I have had far more experience with my own race," one student wrote, and in this experience, "matters of race were largely unaddressed because there was not much of a racial divide." Another student wrote, "A major reason [for my result] is because I have had little contact with African Americans versus European Americans." Others actually took their reflection a step further to move toward action. As one student remarked, "One thing I would like to improve on is my interaction with other cultures in college. I have not done as good of a job at interacting with other cultures as I would like since arriving at JBU." Another student simply said, "I need to travel more."

Assessment Results

Following the intergroup dialogue exercises, students completed the same cultural diversity assessment they had filled out before the exercises. Students showed marked improvement in a few areas of response including:

- "I can honestly assess my strengths and weaknesses in the area of diversity and try to improve myself." (3.5 to 4.4)
- "I assume good intent and ask for clarification when I don't understand what was said or implied." (3.5 to 4.1)
- "I challenge others when they make racial/ethnic/sexually offensive comments or jokes." (3.1 to 3.8)
- "I avoid assuming that others will have the same reaction as me when discussing or viewing an issue." (3.5 to 4.1)
- "I recognize that others stereotype me and I try to overcome their perceptions." (3.1 to 3.9)
- "I actively seek opportunities to connect with people different than me and seek to build rapport." (2.9 to 3.8)
- "I actively convey that nontraditional employees or students are as skilled and competent as others." (3.3 to 4.0)
- "I do not try to justify acts of discrimination to make the victim feel better. I validate his/her assessment of what occurred." (3.1 to 4.3)
- "I believe there are policies and practices in place that negatively impact people outside the majority culture." (3.6 to 4.5)
- "I understand the definition of internalized racism and how it impacts people of color." (3.2 to 4)
- "I believe that race is a social construct, not a scientific fact." (3.5 to 4.5)

One of the more interesting response results came on the statement "I do not take physical characteristics into account when interacting with others and when making decisions about competence or ability." On the pre-assessment responses, *every* student scored themselves perfectly in this area—5 out of 5. On the post-assessment, the average score was 3.8. This can largely be attributed to their experience in discussing implicit bias. Despite students' initial reluctance to accept their results, it was clear that the results had caused students to engage in honest assessment of their own biases.

These were immediate results, but responses from students about seven months later to a follow-up survey reveals that some students experienced lasting impacts from the intergroup dialogue experience. In response to a question about how intergroup dialogue helps them today, some students stated that the experience has given them more tools for difficult discussions. One student wrote, "Being a part of the intergroup dialogue helped me to respond with openness and grace in these situations ["ideological discussion"], especially when I do not agree with the opinion of the other party." Similarly, another student wrote, "I recall our discussions whenever I am talking to someone and they have a vastly different opinion than I. It reminds me that they have reasoning behind their thinking, and that I should value their opinion and consider what angle they are viewing the issue from." These quotes reflect the most common theme in the responses—that of an openness to having conversations across difference and humility in engagement with others.

Limits and Plans for Improvement

Despite long-term positive results for some students, there were limits to the intergroup dialogue experience in this particular setting. The first is that there was little ethnic or racial difference among the students in both sections of the class, which made true intergroup dialogue on race impossible. While the Honors Scholars Program continues to work toward greater ethnic and racial diversity in the program, there are still strong institutional barriers to success in this area. The Honors Scholars Program is currently working with the JBU office of admissions to recruit international students and local Latino students to the HSP. As we work toward greater diversity in our program, we will be better able to provide opportunities for cross-cultural dialogue in the great texts course. The second limit to the great texts/intergroup dialogue course is that the class never provided an opportunity for students to enter into stage four of intergroup dialogue—movement toward action. In the next iteration of the course, the curriculum will include intentional discussions and assignments focused on developing plans of action for the future. These will include partnering with community groups and student organizations on campus that address particular areas of injustice. A good deal of work also needs to be done to prepare majority culture students for the shock they will experience when they receive their results from the implicit bias assessment. Explaining implicit bias and the nature of the assessment before students take the assessment will provide a better foundation for fruitful self-evaluation and dialogue. Finally, while students experienced some transformation from these brief encounters with intergroup dialogue, the fact that it was incorporated into an honors class largely focused on great texts meant that there were significant time barriers involved in planning and implementing the intergroup dialogue experiences. In order to address this, more class time will be devoted to the intergroup dialogue experience.

The curriculum is well worth the investment of the Honors Scholars Program, as it is clear that incorporating intergroup dialogue into the student class experience had immediate and long-lasting impacts on students in the area of cross-cultural engagement. By strengthening the intergroup dialogue experience, the JBU Honors Scholars Program can become a campus leader in helping students develop skills to engage in cross-cultural dialogue in positive and effective ways.

CHAPTER THREE

THE POWER OF CONVERSATION: INCLUSIVE HONORS ADVISING AND STIMULATING STUDENT CREATIVITY

LAURA HANNA

Introduction

I teach interdisciplinary courses at Valdosta State University's Honors College in Valdosta, Georgia. I also advise honors students, helping them navigate the completion of their honors coursework as well as helping them find creative ways to fulfill their other honors requirements (please see Appendix A for a breakdown of specific curricular requirements for VSU's Honors College). Similar to the demographics at other regional honors colleges, our honors student enrollment includes many first-generation college students, students from minority cultures, and students with minority sexual orientations. The Honors College is a welcoming, open environment where students can feel comfortable being themselves and exploring who they are in an academic context. Advising and teaching honors students is a distinctive experience because honors students tend to be self-motivated, high achieving, and highly driven. Thus, instead of trying to help students meet base-line expectations such as passing their classes, my job alternatively involves helping students seek and implement opportunities to push the envelope and excel through internships, experiential learning, and global experiences.

Furthermore, the wide range of educational and experiential experiences (which I discuss in this chapter with regard to academic honors advising) offered by the VSU Honors College provide a space for students to develop professionally, academically, and socially. However, I have found that honors students, particularly freshmen, oftentimes need a little help in re-opening themselves to the creativity and bravery needed to think outside the box. These characteristics often are stifled by the structure and rigidity of the high school setting where students have habitually been conditioned to follow clear and contained sets of rules and expectations for excelling. The Honors College setting provides a move away from that conditioning in that we want students to push the envelope and explore new ideas in surprising and creative ways.

I began advising honors students in fall 2015. Within the first few weeks of my employment, I began noticing that if I allowed them to, students would let me think for them by coming up with an individualized plan for each of them. Such expenditure of intellectual lavor unsustainable, particularly because our Honors College serves over 370 students. Another component of complexity is added when one considers that these hundreds of students all have majors, interests, and career goals that are vastly different: like most Honors Colleges across the United States, our Honors College accommodates students from many walks of life and a diversity of cultures and from an array of academic disciplines.

This chapter was born out of a need to help beginning honors students gain confidence in their creative capabilities and the academic freedom to pursue their curiosities and passions. There is also a need to help the lowerclassmen rely on themselves more instead of so heavily depending on honors advisors to help them come up with ideas and plans of action for their Honors Option, global experience, and experiential learning projects[1] (much like how they often depended on their high school teachers and counselors to provide the parameters of their assignments and how to reach goals). The goal of honors advising is to help students envision how their interests and career goals can be connected back to these requirements and to equip students with the tools to meet these goals.

This chapter provides insight and practical advice for advisors to intersectionally (I am here referring to the adverb form of the word *intersectionality* in the spirit of legal theorist Kimberlé Williams Crenshaw's use of the term) assist honors students in succeeding as independent thinkers and creative trailblazers. The next sections also show the importance of honors advisors because of their unique job as mentors who help create the Honors College (much like the "creating the university" pedagogical approach[2]) for honors students through advising,

---

[1] Please see Appendix B for the honors global experience guidelines, Appendix C for the honors option guidelines, and Appendix D for the embedded service learning and experiential guidelines available to students in the VSU Honors College.

[2] Advisors play an important role in helping students, particularly freshmen, to understand their role in the university and how to hone the skillsets needed to

mentorship, and conversation. In other words, I want to explore how honors colleges can utilize advising as a tool to help create a more creative, intersectional and inclusive environment where students of all academic and professional interests feel welcomed and can develop the tools needed to excel.

Indeed, the Honors College contains so much academic and social diversity that it would be unfeasible to provide advising with intricate details planned out for every student. This chapter discusses the system devised and implemented to streamline the honors advising process to help students from diverse educational, social, and economic backgrounds become more self-reliant and better able to make connections across disciplines, as well as use their academic work to further their future career goals. This chapter also examines how honors college advisors can help students to gain confidence in themselves to take their education into their own hands and be creative with the means through which they fulfill requirements and meet their academic, personal, and professional goals.

Background

One of the problems with providing students with ready-made examples of projects to complete is that though I give the students examples of previous projects that other students completed, I still cannot specifically guide the student with regard to bridging the gap between theory (the goals of the Honors Option or experiential project, which is to help students become creative and innovative thinkers) and practice (completing the project and gaining practice in applying knowledge in ways that are useful for future academic and career goals). In this situation, the advisor should not be like the high school teacher who gives the student a specific, scaffolded assignment with detailed instructions. Instead of being the person who comes up with ideas for bridging gaps between classroom learning and experiential learning (which is better left up to the student's academic advisor), the honors advisor should be the messenger who tells the students what they are required to do for the Honors College to gain credit.

To put the responsibility of idea generation back on the students, I depend on them to tell me what their goals are after graduation, and I then prompt them to tell me what kind of project they would like to

---

become better students. Ultimately, these skillsets translate into the ability to recognize how to succeed in the professional world.

complete to gain experiential credit or Honors Option credit. If the student comes to advising without that knowledge of future goals and an understanding of what is expected of them within their major, this lack of context makes honors advising less fruitful. Self-awareness is vital for students to be able to generate ideas for their honors projects.

Another important factor necessary for students to excel in the Honors College is the bravery to think outside the box and take intellectual risks. After discussing with several students how their high school coursework and projects were structured, I realized that many honors students are still replicating the behaviors they performed in secondary school—they wait for an authority to tell them exactly how to scaffold and make connections between seemingly disparate subjects and activities. This residual phenomenon is especially true for students new to the university setting. Such characteristics are illustrated when many of the new honors students I advise often lack the knowledge-building skillsets necessary to devise a plan for completing honors requirements in a way that will also reflect their interests, future goals, and major curriculum. This problem becomes especially evident when the advisee comes in for honors advising and is majoring in a field that the advisor has no training in or frame of reference for. Students have a major academic advisor to assist them in navigating major coursework so to avoid redundancy, the honors advisor's job should be to go above and beyond the academic advisor's duties.

My job as an honors advisor is to help students make connections between their honors work and their major coursework. When students with widely different majors and goals come in for honors advising, it becomes a challenge to assist them in deepening their learning experiences within their major and making connections to their honors work because the burden falls on the honors advisor to provide examples of projects to help the student understand the objectives of honors and how those goals connect back to honors. The problem is not that the advisor has to provide examples; indeed, these examples help students to understand what is expected of them in the Honors College setting. Instead, one of the problems is that students (out of fear of getting it wrong or out of intellectual laziness) often adapt the advisor's ideas for projects and use them to complete their own requirements instead of innovating their own ideas.

Even when I provide examples outside of the students' field of interest (so as to avoid giving students too much help, the individual advising session still functions more like a hierarchical power structure with an authority figure giving directions rather than the chance to engage in a conversation that generates ideas to propel students' goals forward. Furthermore, instead of thinking for the student and planning the project, the honors advisor should only be helping the student formalize and fine tune ideas into doable projects. Rather than take the front seat in assisting with the preliminary groundwork of identifying goals, identifying how to reach those goals, and finding a professor or mentor to work with the student on the project, the honors advisor should allow the student to complete the bulk of this work (the advisor can help guide the student, of course, particularly newer students) in order to gain experience planning and developing projects that lead to meeting goals. The transition from individual advising to group advising provides a way to implement the goal of helping students become more independent and confident in their honors journey.

The Turning Point

Some of the goals of the Honors College advisors are to encourage students to chart their own paths, to foster an environment for students to come up with unique and individualized ideas to meet their interests, and to guide students in fulfill Honors College curricular requirements. However, honors advisors should also strike a balance between recommending ways to achieve goals during advising and giving students a sense of independence, creativity, and agency regarding how they achieve those goals. If students learn to be imaginative and innovative with how they envision meeting these requirements, they will be better equipped to do so with a frame of reference that assists them in navigating the real world. Too many students do not try jumping to the deep end of the pool, even though they know how to swim. Many wait for advisors to explain what they should do and how they should do it.

After a few weeks into my first advising season, I began to notice how many students depended on me to act as a bridge who gave them an easy access their destination. Specifically, students were asking me for examples of projects they could do, but instead of thinking of their own projects to suit their interests and skillsets, some students, particularly freshmen, used my examples as their projects. In summer 2016, after a year's worth of advising experience and a chance to reflect and discuss with the other honors advisor, we realized we could no longer continue enabling a system whereby students' creativity and autonomy were not at the forefront. We also realized the emphasis needed to be placed on privileging students' intrinsic motivation and desire to make connections across disciplines and complete extra projects for the desire of learning instead of simply checking boxes that indicate they are completing requirements or, worse, accepting examples as directions instead of taking risks by developing innovative projects. To allow students the freedom to decide on and design their honors projects with minimal constraints is to respect and privilege their autonomy as students who desire more than just completing requirements. But the Honors College needed a system to help students achieve that higher level of thinking—to bring together intrinsic motivation and the skillsets (which our honors students clearly have) that allow students to apply that intrinsic motivation in ways that will yield fruit for them academically and professionally and even allow for the possibility of affecting positive change in the local and regional community. The needed improvement in our advising system came about through the development of honors group advising, which is a simple yet effective system that can easily be implemented by other honors colleges.

During advising, advisors should create the Honors College for students and show them that they should try to test the waters and explore their field of study in unique ways. Honors advising, specifically group advising, can be an ideal time to help students develop that kind of thinking. The next sections chart how advisors can solidify such a learning process in a concrete, replicable way through group advising sessions, which are the marriage between individualized advising and creating an environment where student autonomy is privileged.

Students enrolled in the Valdosta State University Honors College are required to come to honors advising at least once per academic year (please see Appendix E for a full description of honors advising guidelines and details about what typically occurs during group advising). In the past, appointments were all individual meetings (lasting 15 minutes per appointment) which students signed up for using a Google Document link that was emailed to all active students in the Honors College. However, this past fall 2016, we decided to change the advising process to include group advising. I will discuss the strategies used in group advising in the next section. But first, background information will be provided regarding the goals of advising sessions and how those goals serve to accelerate student learning through the planning and implementation of interdisciplinary, multicultural, and socially relevant projects.

The Goals of Honors Advising

During honors advising, several key points are discussed. New honors students are given an outline of the courses they are required to complete (as shown in Appendix A), and current honors students are given the chance to fill out the courses they have already completed (students do this on their own during group advising while the advisor fills the sheet in during individual advising). Students are then apprised of the progress they have made so far in completing honors coursework and what they should take in upcoming semesters. One of the ways that students are able to complete their required honors major courses is by completing an Honors Option (which they can repeat for credit as many times as needed). The Honors Option contract provides VSU Honors College students with the ability to take a non-honors course and complete an additional component of work (such as a research project that connects student interest with course topic, to give a common example) in order to accrue honors credit for the course. As shown in the description in Appendix C, to sign up for an Honors Option, the committed student fills in and submits an electronic form after collaborating with the professor of the major-level course to plan the additional enrichment project.

Another component of the honors advising session includes an explanation of the global experience, which is a necessity for all Valdosta State University honors students to complete before graduating with an Honors College seal. This requirement can be fulfilled in many different ways, including a study abroad trip, a semester exchange, interactions with international students through formal weekly meetings, or research projects that contain a multicultural component (please see Appendix B). Although all of the required Honors College coursework and activities provide students with opportunities to strengthen interdisciplinary ways of thinking, the honors experiential components such as the global experience are unique in that they help students connect to the broader subtext of nuanced cultural understanding, both locally and globally. Honors advising is an integral part of ensuring that students are drawing connections between their experiences, their coursework, and their goals.

Group Advising as a Bridge for Achieving Creativity and Inclusion

One of the main benefits of group advising is the collaboration involved—the dialogical conversation that students get to have with their peers. Students are not just sitting in an office across from an advisor, listening to that advisor spout examples of projects past students completed, and the advisor is not sitting there waiting for the student to think of a project they[3] would like to complete. Students are instead discussing with their peers how to get involved and expand their horizons, and they are hearing examples of successful projects and what the students who completed these projects gained as a result of completing them. Thus, instead of being the disseminator of knowledge or the idea creator, my role as the advisor becomes more akin to a moderator of discussion who helps students find their own path through hearing peers discuss projects they completed successfully. This collaborative, relaxed group session also provides students access to the advisor so they can ask questions as they think of them. Furthermore, the group environment provides a way for students to gain knowledge of a wide variety of projects they can complete for honors credit, including social justice projects that help to bridge the gap between the ivory tower and improving society.

I advised students in the VSU Honors College individually for one year before our Honors College switched to group advising. The other advisors and I have found that during individual advising, students' ideas were too dependent on the advisor's approval and too similar to the examples the advisor gave. However, after implementing group advising this past fall 2016, we noticed this more collaborative technique diffuses the authority to allow students to learn about the sorts of projects they can complete from their peers who actually completed the projects and make up their own minds regarding what project they want to take up instead of waiting for the advisor to tell them what to do or merely choosing to replicate an example. We have found that instead of copying their peers' projects, students instead are becoming even more innovative and outdoing their peers' examples, almost as if there is a competition for improving on the previous examples with more innovation and real-world application.

Importantly, when students get to share ideas together instead of listening to the advisor tell them what sorts of projects they could do, the influence of an authority is no longer a factor that could affect students' decision to choose a particular project. This diffusion of authority is important for at least two reasons. First, students are given the freedom to make their own decision about what sort of project they would like to complete instead of a scenario in which students default to obeying an authority. I have found the vast majority of students who do not already

---

[3] In instances where the pronouns "he" or "she" may have historically been used, in this chapter the pronoun "they" is used either as the third person plural pronoun or to indicate singular third-person pronouns (depending on the context of the sentence) in recognition of students who do not identify with gender binary pronouns (i.e., "he" or "she").

know what project they would be interested in (particularly lower classmen) have not yet sharpened their critical thinking and creativity skills enough to brainstorm how to align their undergraduate coursework and experiences to help them achieve their career goals, or even shorter-term goals. This freedom to choose the best individualized project and to be creative is important because honors students (and all post-secondary students, really) should develop their ingenuity, creativity, and innovation to begin meeting advisors halfway with project ideas instead of merely depending on advisors to do this intellectual heavy-lifting.

Secondly, advisors should steer away from telling students what projects they should do because students are not the instruments an advisor or program coordinator should use to push his or her agenda. An implicit (and I would argue dangerous) bias is inherent when an advisor gives students examples of projects that a student can complete for honors credit because if the student accepts uncritically the suggestions of the advisor, the student's autonomy, ingenuity, and creativity are dimmed. Even if the advisor's suggestion is merely a recommendation, there is still an implicit power dynamic at work because the students are used to a system whereby obedience to the authority figure (whether it is a teacher, advisor, or parent) is a rewarded behavior. The advisor should instead be giving the student the tools and critical thinking skillsets necessary to come to his or her own conclusions about what the project should be, based on the student's academic major and career goals.

The sort of reward-based behavior that causes students to take mere suggestions as directions is insidious because it is a residual strategy that many honors students utilized in high school effectively: they were very good at following the teacher's directions and were rewarded for following those directions because they received high grades and high test scores as a result, thus making them prime candidates for acceptance into the Honors College. However, now that they are in the Honors College, students have to be given the tools to escape that mentality. While this strategy may have been effective in helping them learn and excel in the past, this sort of reward-based behavior does not work in the real world because an employer is going to expect employees to be self-sufficient and look for opportunities to excel autonomously, instead of waiting for the employer to directly tell the employee exactly what to do.

Thus, one of the challenges of the honors advisor is to help students move away from that sort of reward mentality and instead allow the creativity they had in childhood resurface in college as an avenue through which to make connections and leaps between seemingly disparate topics and focus on interdisciplinarity. Furthermore, the burden of giving an example to a student for context often results in the student choosing to complete that project because it is often easier to accept a ready-made idea than to blaze a new trail. Group advising thus becomes a useful instrument through which students are given the opportunity to learn how to identify how the choices they make in the short-term using their Honors College curriculum can help align them toward reaching their long-term goals.

In this way, the advisor's role becomes that of a facilitator who helps guide students without directing them. An example of a technique I now use during individual and group advising to guide students while placing the burden of intellectual heavy-lifting on the student is to ask rhetorical questions. Examples of such questions include, "What are some ways you can formalize your passion for analyzing commercials and use it to deepen and enrich your experiences in this marketing course so that you can gain honors credit for the course?" or, "How can you show this hospital that your interest and background in connecting your studies of biology and chemistry would make you a prime candidate to shadow the microbiology team?" or, "How can you best represent the experiences on your resume or e-portfolio to strengthen your chances of acceptance into graduate school?" Such questions open the door to deeper conversations, the enrichment of experiences, and the scaffolding of knowledge. Furthermore, such questions help prompt students to align their thinking toward metacognition and real-world application of their studies, which in turn become more significant to students beyond the mere attainment of course credit. Equally important, when such questions are posed in the collaborative group advising setting, students' understandings become more fruitful and compounded when they are able to have a conversation with their peers.

The VSU Honors College is continuing to improve the advising process through the organization of the advising sessions based on student major or discipline area instead of just having students sign up for group advising sessions solely based on time and date. This idea came about because several students suggested it in the advising questionnaire we ask students to complete after every group advising session (please see Appendix F to view this questionnaire). We implemented this technique in the fall 2017 semester by creating columns for different majors so that when students signed up for advising, they are able to choose an advising session more closely related to their discipline instead of just choosing a time slot (please see Appendix G for an example advising sign-up sheet).

This revised group advising method is an improvement because when students are grouped by disciplinary area (for example, students who are in the sciences can opt to sign up to be advised with other science-based majors), they will likely have a similar frame of reference that will help to generate conversations that lead to fruitful Honors Options and experiential learning projects that are directly or indirectly beneficial to their future goals. In other words, freshman and sophomore biology or chemistry majors can gain a frame of reference for examples of past successful projects by listening to their older peers who are in similar disciplines talking about the projects they completed for honors credit. Thus, the older students become the authorities on the topic (and mentors of sorts), as opposed to the more generally knowledgeable honors advisor, and can provide more of a context for younger students trying to navigate their field of interest. The advisor in this setting becomes the expert facilitator and communicator of honors requirements, as well as the moderator who organizes the different conversations and activities that will occur during the advising session.

Furthermore, the organization of the advising sessions based on academic area of interest transforms the group advising environment into an incubator for the creation of ideas through discussion instead of a place where the authority figure (the advisor) transmits information and ideas to the advisee. This way of organizing advising is also valuable because students in similar disciplines and majors are likely to have a significant amount of information they can share with their fellow classmates, such as the names of professors who are points of contact for completing Honors Option and experiential learning contracts. Another good reason to engage in group discussions is to give the upperclassmen a chance to teach their younger, less experienced peers about the projects they completed, thus prompting the older students to learn how to articulate the importance of the project to different audiences. Honors students who still have not decided on a major but who know which general area they are interested in can also benefit from this group advising set up because they can get a taste of the kinds of projects students in several related fields of study have completed and may gain a better sense of direction regarding what they may want to major in.

Future Plans for Continued Inclusion and Conclusion

In future semesters, we also plan to add a couple of advising sessions to give the option for first-generation college students to be advised in a group together. Such a setting may be advantageous to students in this situation because they all have a common position as students whose parents did not have the chance to attend college. Such a meeting provides an environment for students to discuss the honors experience, honors goals, and the honors curriculum with peers who are also experiencing college from a common frame of reference. We also are considering the possibility of group advising sessions for first or second generation Americans so that these students can feel a stronger sense of community with students whose frame of reference and experiences in a new culture are similar to theirs.

In conclusion, helping students attain a broader and deeper frame of mind for the goals of honors is important for the improvement of the honors learning experience. One of the most important goals of honors advising experience is to help students increase creativity and innovation with their honors projects and to enrich and enhance their undergraduate experience instead of merely help them complete a list of requirements. To that end, one of the benefits of having group advising is that such a cooperative environment allows students to collaborate, discuss, and explore recent projects in a way that allows for crossover, connection making, and dialogical conversations. Such multi-faceted perspectives and idea generation would not be possible in a one-student advising session. The group advising session allows for the best and the brightest to be in a room together and gives them the chance to bounce ideas off of each other in a think tank that is not hierarchical in structure but instead fosters a conversation meant to help students develop their own individualized avenues toward reaching goals rather than depending on the advisor to do so for them.

Appendix A: Honors Curriculum Requirements

HONORS COLLEGE
Program Requirements

Name _____

Student ID _____

*Advisor*_____

Year Accepted into Honors _____

Programs of Study

INTERDISCIPLINARY Program Requirements	Completed Requirement
• HONS 1990 – 2 credit hours	
• PERSPECTIVE Honors – 2 credit hours	
• Honors Core class – 3 credit hours	
• Honors Core class – 3 credit hours	
• Honors Core or Major class – 3 credit hours	
• Honors Major class – 3 credit hours	
• Honors Major class – 3 credit hours	
• HONS 3990 or 3999 – 3 credit hours	
• HONS 4990 – 3 credit hours	
• GLOBAL EXPERIENCE Requirement	
• 3.3 GPA*	
TOTAL HOURS 24-28	

Program Goals
   1. Scholarship and Research
   2. Service Learning
   3. Interdisciplinarity
   4. Leadership
   5. Global Experience and Understanding

List of personal objectives/goals related to Honors (Advisor notes)

Appendix B: Honors College Global Experience Description

Note: This description can be found on the VSU Honors webpage, linked here: https://www.valdosta.edu/colleges/honors/forms/global-experience.php. Typical examples of projects that would fulfill the global experience requirement include: study abroad, semester exchange, language partners (which entails pairing up with an international student once a week to discuss culture and language), independent or group research, field experience, or a minor degree program in a foreign language.

Honors Global Experience Requirement

All students in the Honors College must complete the Global Experience and Understanding requirement through an approved research activity, service learning assignment, or field experience. The semester-long commitment fosters understanding of global and cultural issues. In the spirit of the interdisciplinary approach of the Honors College, research, service, and minor degree program activities will be considered. These activities must be approved by the Honors College.

Global learning is a critical analysis of and an engagement with complex, interdependent global systems and legacies (such as natural, physical, social, cultural, economic, and political) and their implications for people's lives and the earth's sustainability. Through global learning, students should 1) become informed, open-minded, and responsible people who are attentive to diversity across the spectrum of differences, 2) seek to understand how their actions affect both local and global communities, and 3) address the world's most pressing and enduring issues collaboratively and equitably. (AACU, 2015)

To provide guidance for the Global Experience projects or activities, students should review and reference the Center for Strategic and International Studies (CSIS), Seven Revolutions Program. The CSIS program is a research effort to identify and analyze important trends shaping our world. Any project or activity used to satisfy the Global Experience requirement should connect to one of these themes. For additional information on the 7R program: http://csis.org/program/seven-revolutions

The Global Experience projects and activities should also connect to global learning outcomes established by the American Association of Colleges and Universities (AAC&U). The AAC&U VALUE Rubrics were developed by teams of experts to provide fundamental criteria for learning outcomes. The Global Learning rubric (available in the Honors College) is useful in determining the merit and criteria for a useful global experience activity or project.   For additional information on AAC&U's Global Learning projects: http://www.aacu.org/resources/global-learning

Appendix C: Honors Option Description

Honors Option Contract

The Honors Option is designed to enable students to take courses not designated as Honors. The following guidelines apply to Honors Option Contracts:

- Honors Option Contracts are intended for Major courses where no Honors courses are designated.
- Honors Option Contracts are not intended for Core courses. Students should take scheduled Honors designated courses. Honors Option Contracts for core classes will be considered in extenuating circumstances.
- Students are responsible for coordinating with the instructor of the course before submitting the Honors Option Contract.
- To receive Honors credit, enhanced assignments or activities must be clearly and specifically outlined in the Honors Option Contract.
- Honors Option Contracts must be submitted no later than the second week of classes.
- All specified work must be satisfactorily completed by the end of the semester with the instructors' confirmation.
- Students must receive a B or higher to receive credit for Honors.

Rationale for an Honors Contract

It is important to stress that the Honors Option Contract is about quality not quantity of work. The important distinction of an Honors course is that it is an enhanced experience generally completed outside of the regular class setting.

This contract must be submitted electronically no later than the end of the second week of classes. Successful Honors Options require planning, and most students begin the process during pre-registration. The more lead time a professor has, the greater the opportunity to integrate the student's personal research interests and the professor's goals for the course.

Honors Option enhanced activities must include:

- A direct connection to one or more of the four Honors foundations of scholarship, interdisciplinarity, leadership, and/or service learning. All projects must specifically indicate the relationship to one or more of these principles.

- A direct connection to the selected educational outcomes for Honors.
- The possibility for submission to academic conferences such as the VSU Undergraduate Research Symposium.

Timeline for Honors Option Contracts

Students should meet with the professor during advising to establish specific goals and mentoring for the activity. Honors Option Contracts are meant to build these relationships and not to engage students solely in additional academic work.

In the first two weeks of the semester, Honors Option Contracts must be submitted with a detailed description of the activity including the connection to one or more of our foundational principles and educational outcomes.

Once the contract is approved, students must complete the work two weeks before the end of the semester. It is the students' responsibility to submit the work that has been assessed and approved by the course instructor.

Upon successful completion of the terms listed above, the Honors designation will be placed on the student transcript.

Appendix D: Honors College Service and Experiential Learning Contract Description

Note: This description can be found on the VSU Honors webpage, linked here: https://www.valdosta.edu/colleges/honors/forms/honors-service-and-experiential-learning-contract-.php. Typical examples of service and experiential learning projects include: community outreach, study abroad or semester exchange, career shadowing, internship, research activity, leadership activity, or creative activity or performance.

Service and Experiential Learning Contract

The Honors Service Learning contract is required of all Honors Scholars service projects and for students engaged in Experiential Learning Projects. Please review the guidelines carefully to ensure that your project/activity will be approved.

Service learning connects classroom curriculum with service projects. This is achieved through community-based education and civic engagement. It engages students in projects that serve multiple communities in building social, civic, and academic skills.

"Service learning is a pedagogical strategy, not an outcome. Service learning is an opportunity for students to learn 21st century skills through project development, implementation, and reflection: Collaboration, Communication, Critical Thinking/Problem Solving, and Creativity. Research demonstrates when students participate in high quality service-learning we see positive academic, social/emotional, and civic outcomes." (Service Learning, CPS, 2013)

Appendix E: Advising Guidelines

Note: This description can be found on the VSU Honors webpage, linked here: https://www.valdosta.edu/colleges/honors/forms/advising.php.

Honors Advising Guidelines

The Honors College strongly encourages students to attend honors advising sessions at least once per academic year to ensure their satisfactory progression toward completion of their Honors requirements. These sessions provide students an opportunity to review their standing in the program and discuss ideas for Honors core courses, Honors Options, service learning, and global experiences. Advising also provides students with a space to explore connections between coursework and collegiate experiences for the final Honors portfolio.

Students should be aware that Honors advising does not replace academic advising. It is the student's responsibility to ensure that they are planning and completing the Honors College requirements effectively. If a student enters the Honors College already having completed some core requirements, then he or she should discuss with an Honors advisor flexible and creative ways to catch up. Honors advisors are here to help facilitate a plan of action to help all students complete Honors requirements satisfactorily.

We want all of our students to complete as many of the other honors requirements as possible before taking Honors 3990/9 and 4990. Therefore, long-term planning is essential to prevent an Honors course overload. Listed below are helpful guidelines to help keep you on track. Make sure to look ahead and prepare for requirements in future semesters.

First and Second Year Students

In your first and second years in the Honors College, you should consider the following questions:

- Are you coming to Honors advising at least once per academic year?
- Are you taking at least one Honors core course per semester?
- Have you taken Honors 1990 and an Honors PERS course?

- Have you thought about the following key Honors objectives and how to plan to fulfill them?
  - o Global experience
  - o Honors Options
  - o Service learning
  - o Leadership
  - o Research
- Are you thinking about and writing about the connections between your Honors courses activities and your other college experiences? Save this writing and reflection for your Honors e-portfolio.
- Are you using Honors work as a vehicle through which to traverse, build on, and expand your academic interests and passions?
- Are you participating in at least one new activity per semester? Are you documenting these experiences in your resume and/or curriculum vitae?
- We hope students are going outside their comfort zones and exploring the opportunities available to them in order to gain experience beyond the classroom setting. For example, students should actively consider:

  - o Taking on leadership roles
  - o Presenting at academic conferences (especially with the Honors College)
  - o Volunteering
  - o Involvement with the Honors Student Association
  - o Collaborating with other students on academic projects

Third and fourth Year Students

In your third and fourth years in the Honors College, you should consider the following questions:

- Have you been and are you still coming to Honors advising at least once per academic year?
- Have you completed your Honors core requirements?
- Are you completing your Honors major course requirements through Honors Options or Experiential learning?
- Are you aligning yourself to be finished with Honors requirements by the time of your graduation?

- Have you fulfilled (or are you finishing up) the following key Honors objectives?
  o Global experience
  o Honors Options
  o Service learning
  o Leadership opportunities
  o Internships
  o Undergraduate research
- Have you been reflecting on these experiences and how they have contributed to your overall professional, academic, and personal development?
- Can you articulate how your involvements in the Honors College have been effective to those ends? You should be writing about your reflections so that you will have artifacts that show evidence of development to place in your e-portfolio.
- Are you scheduled to complete Honors 3990/9 and Honors 4990 before graduating?
- https://www.valdosta.edu/colleges/honors/forms/certification-application.php

To sign up for group advising, please follow this link:
https://docs.google.com/spreadsheets/d/1jFj0D8wXhZsfKcRHjaC9rasueP
pOu1levJP8fn0cM7E/edit
- Have you filled out the Honors graduation application?
If you have any questions about advising, send us an email at: honors@valdosta.edu.

Advising Options

Group advising:
Group advising is meant to help all Honors students maximize their time in the Honors College by completing coursework and other requirements effectively. Students should come get advised at least once per academic year, but preferably once per semester. Advising is important to help students ensure they are making adequate progress toward receiving their Honors seal and graduating on time.

Information about group advising:

15-20 people per session
- Advising happens in the Honors House
- Begins the third week of September and runs through the first week of November in the fall
- Begins the third week of February and runs through the first week of April in the spring
- BRING YOUR MOST RECENT TRANSCRIPT or electronic device to pull up transcript AND pencil and paper

Individual advising
Individual advising is for students who cannot attend group advising or who have further questions after group advising. Individual advising sessions will be set up on a case-by-case basis.

Appendix F: Group Advising Questionnaire

Note: This questionnaire is an electronic form we ask students to fill out after getting advised. The form itself can be found at the following URL: https://www.valdosta.edu/colleges/honors/forms/advising.php. Completed and submitted forms are sent to an electronic folder in the honors advisors' email inboxes.

ADVISING QUESTIONNAIRE INSTRUCTIONS

Fill out the form and submit at the end of your advising session. This document is part of the advising process and will be an artifact in the Honors e-portfolio.

NAME _____

STUDENT ID_____

1. What are your career goals? Are you satisfied with these goals and your progress toward them? *

2. How have you been working with faculty, staff, and community leaders to develop strong professional networks and relationships that might lead to recommendation and opportunities? If you have not, what can you do to improve? *

3. Over the course of the past academic year, have you grown professionally, academically, and personally? Reflect and write about your progression. *

4. What experiences in the Honors College have been most enriching for your development? Do you feel that you can be creative in meeting your academic, personal, and professional goals in Honors? How can Honors help you? Be certain to document your progress and explain why the experiences are meaningful. *

5. How can we alter the Honors experience to help you achieve your goals? (Examples include Honors Option Contracts, curriculum, professors, activities, etc.) *

Appendix G: Example Advising Sign-Up Sheet

Note: The advising sign-up sheet is usually created using a Google Document that is editable by anyone with the link to allow honors students to sign up for honors advising. This link is available on the honors advising page on the VSU Honors website so that it is easily accessible and editable to students. There are three advisors in the Honors College who are able to advise the three different groups of students at any one time. For the sake of example, a sample day of the advising sign-up sheet that will be used in fall 2017 is provided in this appendix. The advising sessions are grouped based on major so that each advising session can cater to a common disciplinary area, such as the humanities or the math and sciences. This way, students in each advising session will have a common frame of reference from which to discuss examples and experiences.

Honors Group Advising Sign-Up Sheet

Directions: Please sign up for advising by putting your name in one of the time slots below. We would prefer that you sign up for advising based on your discipline, but if the times available for your discipline do not work with your schedule, you can sign up for a time that works regardless of your major. If your major is undecided, attend the advising session that most closely matches your interests. Your changes will automatically be saved since this is a Google Document. Be careful not to alter anyone else's information. Time slots that are blacked out mean you cannot sign up for that particular time. You can expect the advising session to last from 45 minutes to an hour.

Date	Business	Humanities (History, English, Psychology, etc.)	Science (Chemistry, Biology, Geosciences, etc.)	Math (Math Physics, Computer Science, etc.)	Education and Nursing Majors
Feb. 28 @ 9am					

Feb. 28 @ 1pm					
Feb. 28 @ 6pm					

CHAPTER FOUR

UBUNTU AND THE NEED
FOR COMPLEMENTARITY
IN HONORS EDUCATION

GRAEME HARPER

Honors' Interdependence

"The profound truth is," says Desmond Tutu, speaking of the Nguni Bantu term Ubuntu (*oo-boon-too*), "you cannot be human on your own."[1] "We are made for complementarity." Ubuntu, to which Tutu strongly adheres, became better known worldwide as a philosophy in the 1990s during South Africa's transition from apartheid to democracy. Ubuntu advocates that we are human because we participate in relationships. In speaking at the Nelson Mandela Memorial Service about Mandela and his life, Barack Obama used the word and ideal of Ubuntu to focus on what he called "Mandela's greatest gift". Mandela's profound commitment to Ubuntu, Obama said, included his recognition "that we achieve ourselves by sharing ourselves with others."[2]

"We achieve ourselves by sharing ourselves with others" – a challenging statement for college honors education not because honors programs and colleges fail to include service to others (we do indeed actively embrace such service), or because honors programs and colleges do not embody ideals of community (we most certainly speak regularly of community and of communities, of shared ideals and of positive common goals), or because we do not wish to share and promote laudable ideals of aspiration, commitment, diligence, intention and engagement. Rather, "we achieve ourselves by sharing ourselves with others" is a challenging statement for honors educators because of our often-declared selectivity,

---

[1] Desmond Tutu, https://www.youtube.com/watch?v=0wZtfqZ271w (2013)
[2] Barack Obama, https://www.youtube.com/watch?v=2KzGZyO_lSU (2016)

commonly based on a bedrock of prior individual academic achievement. That prior individual academic achievement, and its manifestation in college honors, is further bound up in declarations of and belief in distinctiveness. It is entwined with ideals of exceptionality. And it ultimately projects future reward and ultimately rites and rights of celebrating certain types of achievement. In this regard, the National Collegiate Honors Council (NCHC) Board of Directors approved "Definition of Honors Education" states that honors education involves

> . . . in-class and extracurricular academic experiences that provide a distinctive learning environment for *selected students.*[3] *– my italics.*

"Distinctive" is used here not only to suggest difference but to affirm educational quality, a selective reward associated with defined and then celebrated "academic" achievements. Further, in that same document:

> In most cases, the honors community is composed of carefully selected teachers and students who form a cross or multi-disciplinary cohort dedicated to achieving exceptional learning and personal standards.[3]

Again, the expression "exceptional learning and personal standards" is not a generic reference to universally agreed perceptions and conditions of merit – rather, it contains aggregated political, economic and cultural intention and meaning. Such intention and meaning, as it pertains to honors education, could be said to be part of a narrowly focused meritocracy, whereby certain forms of knowledge, certain types of achievement, certain personal and group ideals, goals and outcomes are always deemed more worthy than others.

If indeed honors education is truly about "broader, deeper, and more complex learning-centered and learner-directed experiences" the compound question therefore becomes what this learning might be in its "learner-centered" and "learner-directed" experiences, who the learners will be, and to what real ends are these learning experiences offered and undertaken? With this in mind, is it actually possible to have equity in

---

[3] National Collegiate Honors Council, 'Definition of Honors Education' NCHC Board of Directors,
https://www.nchchonors.org/uploaded/NCHC_FILES/PDFs/Definition-of-Honors-Education.pdf (2013)

honors education? If not, then on what basis can inequity be acceptable in a genuinely principled college honors college or program?

Let me be clear, I am not saying here that honors education or honors educators (and I am primarily speaking of honors education in the USA here) can singlehandedly resolve widespread issues of educational inequality, within the nation or within culture, or across nations and cultures. Nor am I accusing honors education or honors educators of being complacent or apathetic with regard to supporting equity, and the attendant conditions of diversity and inclusion. It is not being suggested here, either, that individual and group attainment should *not* be rewarded and should *not* be celebrated. Quite the opposite: every human celebration is potentially empathetic, a public recognition of human achievements that bring us and bind us together as people, showing our profound complementarity. However, what I am saying is that at the heart of the humanity so often alluded to in honors education, and so frequently touted by dedicated and often passionate honors educators, a humanity founded on the importance of learning and human understanding and a belief in such things as community, such things as shared aspirations, such things as the pursuit of nonpartisan excellence, lies a spirit tethered by epistemological notions that, at least at the site of discernible action, appear to serve political and economic means more than they serve a more broadly human ideal of "honors". As Desmond Tutu suggests "we are made for [the] delicate network of interdependence, *inter*-dependence". (Tutu: 2013) We might ask if in US college honors education such interdependence is yet strong enough; whether, in pursuing distinctiveness, declaring exceptionality, promoting future reward and ultimately celebration of types of knowledge and types of excellence, we have failed to deal as well as we can, and should, with that key human trait: complementarity. Ponder this:

> A recent report of the European Monitoring Centre on Racism and Xenophobia (EMCRX) indicated that the educational achievements of migrants and ethnic minorities lagged behind that of the majority groups, with many facing high rates of underachievement that limit their future employment opportunities and negatively impact on their livelihood (EMCRX, 2004). Whilst the root causes are complex, it appears that inadequate pedagogical approaches, ethnic

discrimination in educational institutions, and inequalities in
society contribute to this situation.[4]

"High rates of underachievement" is an expression that will naturally
alarm any educator. This EMCRX report is referring to conditions in
Europe, but the American story aches with similarity. With high rates of
underachievement an individual's life chances are diminished, people and
their communities are weakened; generally, education and educators
naturally consider they are failing learners. All three noted aspects spring
out as related to discussions of diversity, equity and inclusion in college
honors education because they are topics honors educators have frequently
considered in honors courses and more widely in extra- and co-curricular
honors activities: "inequalities in society", "ethnic discrimination in
educational institutions" and "inadequate pedagogical approaches". Unlike
Europe, however, in America honors programs and honors colleges have
long embraced direct social/service purpose, have long declared a
programmatic interest in civic responsibility and in social justice. The
situation is not the same in a country like, say, the United Kingdom where
undergraduate students most commonly do graduate with "honors" (for
example, BA [Hons], BSc [Hons]), rather than with "ordinary degrees",
but any programmatic commitment to community service is marginal at
most. Similarly, an interest in social justice and understanding might be
inferred, but individual and program outcomes in the UK rarely lay claim
to contributing to it as a program objective, as they frequently do in the
American honors education. For example, from a student at Florida's
Miami Dade College:

> The opportunities that have been made available to me are
> astounding. For example, I completed over 10 hours of
> community service for one of my Honors courses this
> semester. By working with individuals with intellectual
> disabilities, I became more understanding of what life is like
> for them and found that we are more similar than I had
> previously thought.[5]

Again, my aim is not to point the finger at honors educators in the USA
and declare: "we have failed to adequately address questions raised about

---

[4] Robin Richardson, *Race Equality and Education: A Practical Resource for the
School Workforce* (London: Association of Teachers and Lecturers, 2005): 6.
[5] Laurie Charles in "The Value of Honors Education", National Collegiate Honors
Council, http://www.nchcguide.com/about-nchc/value-honors-education/

diversity, equity and inclusion". But it is to say that the history and development of US college honors education holds a particular place and distinction in the world, and the leverage it offers for addressing questions of diversity, equity and inclusion in education and perhaps more widely in society is entwined with that honors history and development. Here in the USA, in pursuit of support of gifted and high achieving students, honors education has embraced not only personal achievement but also ideals that clearly purport to support social and communal advances. "Awareness of and sensitivity to social class, economic class, ethnicity and gender have been important goals of the academy and of honors for the past few decades," wrote William Ashton, the director of an honors program at a public college in Queens, NYC in 2009. He concluded:

> We are left with two conflicting needs. Honors programs create more careful and complex thinkers when they have students in the program who strongly and confidently espouse their different perspectives on life. However, honors may be a risky luxury these students cannot afford. Our programs derive essential benefits from the participation of students from the lower economic classes while the benefits to these students are fraught with risk. I cannot offer a solution to this dilemma, but awareness of it may help us design and maintain better honors programs.[6]

Ashton is flagging another aspect of diversity strategy that further emphasizes the complexity of the issue – without, as he notes offering "a solution to this dilemma". Six years earlier, Peter J. Longo and John Falconer, like Ashton writing in the *Journal of the National Collegiate Honors Council,* wrote: "Public regional universities and state colleges are often the most accessible institutions for minority students. Accessibility does not always match with the construct of a selective honors program."[7] Longo and Falconer continued: "Honors programs could dramatically enrich their academic environments by better reflecting the diverse nature of society, which provides valuable challenges to students."[8] And further: ". . . the political and educational systems together deliver the opportunities for new peoples to access the promise of America. While

---

[6] William A. Ashton, "Honors needs diversity more than the diverse need honors*." Journal of the National Collegiate Honors Council*, vol. 10, no. 1, (2009): 67.

[7] Peter J. Longo and John Falconer, "Diversity opportunities for higher education and honors programs: a view from Nebraska", *Journal of the National Collegiate Honors Council*. 4.1, Spring-Summer, (2003): 53.

[8] Longo and Falconer (2003): 54.

education empowers, empowerment must navigate through political realities to reach all citizens."[9]

Such evidence, which is indicative of much more evidence over time, suggests this discussion has had a great deal of formal recognition in American honors education – perhaps, we must now be saying, for far too long. As with many things that persist, it could well be that underlying formative and intrinsic assumptions, abstractions and suppositions are to blame for what is occurring rather than conspicuous action. So, we have approached solutions through addressing what appears to be in front of us, but what actually has impelled and perpetuated the scene has been left largely intact. The fear is that the approach taken, so far, has therefore merely chipped away at the surface of the issue, rather than dealt with core structural and systemic needs; that while we might in some ways have addressed diversity, equity and inclusion, without closer address to formative and intrinsic assumptions we won't actually challenge inequity.

That thought is as blunt as it is concerning. It leads me to suggest that the only principled kind of honors education, the only honors education than can possibly reach its declared desire to truly contribute to both individual and societal improvement is an interdependent honors education, an honors education based on what Desmond Tutu, referencing to Ubuntu, would call "complementarity". What therefore follows is exploration of some aspects of the philosophy of Ubuntu, as envisaged in future college honors education in the USA.

Creating and Supporting Horizontal Leadership

The leadership model most commonly associated with honors is vertical. It is a pyramidal model where such things as grade point average (GPA), in particular, along with extra credit strategies, awards for notable honors projects and theses, and even recognition of superior contributions to community service present a hierarchy of achievement that places leadership on a rung rather than as a distributed human force. However, there are many models of leadership that are equally if not more successful. The model obviously in contrast to the pyramidal or vertical model is that most often described as "horizontal". Horizontal or collaborative leadership is networked and dynamic. Horizontal or collaborative leadership in this case involves not separating honors education from the rest of campus but placing it in a network of connections and support, whether programmatic, connected with research

---

[9] Longo and Falconer (2003): 55.

or related to service activities. The network extends further than this too in utilizing the visible conditions of the institution to promote interdependence. Thus, collaborative spaces are preferred over separate honors residences, honors recognition of the variety of attainments on campus is another key component (for example, departmental honors, but also outstanding athletics, contributions to philanthropy, outstanding community engagement across the institution), honors celebrating achievement most widely.

These approaches can include the honors college/program formal management of such institutional activities as undergraduate research for students and faculty across the campus and the launching of campus-wide awards and celebrations, managed by the honors college or program but available to all, and the creation of programmatic choices within an honors college or program that allows for empowerment of disciplinary expertise, both of students and of faculty. Horizontal leadership is about both self-reliance and about co-reliance. In the spirit of Ubuntu, it is in this way recognized that without you I cannot be me, without your success I cannot truly achieve my success.

Horizontal leadership can also be thought of as based on a deeper and more empathetic understanding of team dynamics. A productive example of how such an understanding of team dynamics can work is that offered by Meredith Belbin,[10] whose analysis of teams identifies networked team roles and contributions and considers behavioral traits that highlight individual contributions and roles in leading aspects of any team's success. Each role has a purpose with the networked team and each individual has a contribution to make.

Because of the considerable logistical labor and, quite simply, the cost of studying the behaviours of *all* students at *all* times, the "Belbin Team Role Inventory" might not be practically employed to construct a horizontal leadership plan across an institution. Figuratively, however, it provides a useful model for valuing individual traits and for recognizing that a team, and the individuals within it, achieves most when personal behaviours and therefore strengths are supported and capitalized upon. Belbin's list of team roles is as follows:

1. Implementer
2. Shaper
3. Plant
4. Monitor-Evaluator

---

[10] R. Meredith Belbin, *Management Teams: Why They Succeed or Fail* (London; Heinemann, 1981).

5. Resource Investigator
6. Team Worker
7. Specialist
8. Coordinator
9. Completer-Finisher.[11]

It is beyond the scope of the analysis here to delve extensively into what Belbin means by each of these role definitions. However, as examples, a "team worker" is said to be good at encouraging cooperation and a "completer-finisher" ensures timely completion of tasks. Beyond these specifics, horizontal leadership strategies and concerted analyses of team dynamics, like that analyses offered by Meredith Belbin, highlight that all human beings have strengths and weaknesses. When each human strength is recognized and capitalized upon we as a species are more successful, we as cultures and societies are more robust, and we as individuals are more fulfilled.

In honors colleges and programs we so often talk about community, communities of learners and teachers and about contributing to the wider community. Considering of team roles is instructive, in highlighting truths about human interdependence and complementarity within all communities. A strategic investment in interdependence and complementarity is a commitment to diversity and inclusion, because both interdependence and complementarity are clearly made stronger by comprehensive and robust networks. This is not to take away from honors education our ability to pursue individual excellence, innovation, personal leadership or deep learning and engagement; in fact, such an investment is more in tune with doing exactly that because it is located in the ways in which humankind actually thrives. As Tutu notes: "you cannot be human on your own."[12.] Each separation or division or disconnection within a network weakens that network, so recognizing and maintaining connections is tantamount to building a foundation for success.

A horizontal leadership approach does not ignore the influence of politics, economics and mainstream culture on education, or the ways in which we individually strive to succeed not only for others but for ourselves. However, it does make the pursuit of equity a condition of a deeper and more empathetic understanding of human dynamics, and that understanding is surely fundamental for achieving "exceptional learning and personal standards."

---

[11] http://www.belbin.com/about/belbin-team-roles/
[12] Desmond Tutu, https://www.youtube.com/watch?v=0wZtfqZ271w (2013).

Curricula Ubuntu: Types of Knowledge

Expertise is culturally defined as well as defined by fields and types of human endeavor. While commonsense guides us toward some universal truths, the impact of social and personal backgrounds has consequences for what we believe to be justifiable, truthful and real. This is the case whether that knowledge is *a priori* or *a posteriori,* because logic and abstraction as well as empirical investigation is influenced by social group, individual and group background, belief and context. One example could be that an expert in what has often been defined as "Eastern" medicine might not be recognized as an expert in what has similarly defined as "Western" medicine, but both are considered by their adherents as being valid medical approaches and both influence not only individual choices but group and societal choices as well. A less balanced example is explored in Britt Rusert's 2017 book*, Fugitive Science: Empiricism and Freedom in Early African American Culture* (NYU) in which Rusert chronicles a 19th century counter-movement by a group of black writers, artists, and performers to the weighty influence of scientific racism. She writes:

> More than simply establishing the fact of black humanity, African Americans used natural science to profoundly mediate on the category of the human itself – on its possibilities, limits, and its complex relationship to blackness, a concept that exceeds a simply biological or even transparently empirical relationship to race.[13]

Rusert's skill here is in recognizing that such a counter-movement is not solely a minority response to the majority but a determined returning to and reconsideration of entrenched (and in her example, entrenching) perceptions – and a challenge to these on a deeper and more universally significant level. In this sense, acknowledging a greater range and more types of knowledge is not unambiguously a way of enhancing college honors education with a smattering of courses that reflect diverse backgrounds and alternative views. In fact, doing so in that way might well further entrench an inequitable relationship in a way that detracts from the potential for the greater positive impact of honors.

  An honors college or program constructed around a liberal arts ideal, where there is an exposure to varieties of human understanding, can

---

[13] Britt Rusert, *Fugitive Science: Empiricism and Freedom in Early African American* Culture (New York: NYU press, 2017): 6.

either simply touch upon epistemological diversity or it can seek to embrace and articulate epistemological choices and reflect directly on alternate ontologies. In the former what is presented is the mere appearance of inclusion; in the latter, there is the potential for recognizing and articulating an ontology of interdependence and complementarity that ultimately benefits both individual and society.

Curricula Ubuntu recognizes knowledge as based on context, culture and belief; while at the same time offering a constructive model with wide pedagogic implications – the kind that the National College Honors Council appears to be suggesting in its many statements on the nature of honors education. After all, what we are surely talking about here is the principled creating of "broader, deeper, and more complex learning-centered and leaner-directed experiences"[14] alternative – that is, a curriculum based on a kind of industrial utility – is more likely to embed inequity and uniformity, and while that might serve a political and economic purpose it turns honors education, with its declarations of "exceptional learning and personal standards" into the gas that only turns one particular kind of engine.

Honors for Our Synaptic World

Today we live in a networked digital world. In this enormous contemporary network, which is not available to everyone on Earth equally but is nevertheless the most comprehensive in our human history, there are synapses where we cross one or more points in time, one or more place, one or more site of expertise and/or experience, one or more personal histories, one or more cultures. These "crossings", while virtual, have impacted significantly on our interpersonal relations. This is reflected in our increased use of, some might even say "dependence on", social media; in our ability to respond to others in multiple modes, often combining voice, moving image, and still image; and in our employing of newly accessible versions and combinations of actual, virtual and augmented communication. Because of the speed at which information and experiences are recorded and exchanged it seems clear that this contemporary digital revolution has also had an impact on our cognitive functions – with our reception, processing, analysis and responding to

---

[14] National Collegiate Honors Council, 'Definition of Honors Education' NCHC Board of Directors, https://www.nchchonors.org/uploaded/NCHC_FILES/PDFs/Definition-of-Honors-Education.pdf (2013)

events and ideas, both near and far; through the challenging of old modes of attention along with our ability to reason from and about what we see and hear; and in shifting the role and responsiveness of memory as stimuli arrive today in such a rapid and eclectic manner. It has also impacted on our use of language. Certainly text-messaging is nothing if it is not a new form of written language. But the impact on language is greater than texting, in that contemporary digital synapses demand new forms of knowledge, available at short notice and exchangeable over a range of individual and group interactions.

An honors education for such a new synaptic world would use and celebrate space, time, eclecticism and, indeed, diversity more effectively than we see happening in current honors colleges and programs. If contemporary honors education is truly providing "a distinctive learning environment" it would take these new conditions and use and initiate synapses to identify ways in which honors education can contribute to and be relevant to such a world . Here today is "a distinctive learning environment" because it has never existed in this form before. With that in mind, a practical response as well as one that is reflective of what Tutu has called "a delicate network of interdependence", would at least include some of the following:

- an increase in the number of honors courses conducted synchronously across the world, using time and space and diverse knowledge and experience in ways never before seen to accomplish tasks in real/synchronous and asynchronous time where what is attempted and achieved is made stronger by the new networked environments in which we live;
- more exchange between geographically spread programs and a range of student as well as faculty perspectives rather than the persistence of individualized, non-networked programs and colleges, largely hierarchically structured. This greater exchange taking diversity to be enhanced by interdependence and taking knowledge to be most exchangeable when not limited by a narrow delineation of ownership; but, rather, empowered by collaborative exchange, as modelled by contemporary digitalism, of which social media is one pervasive component;
- rather than digital media merely producing a course choice or an add-on to the overall shape of an honors college or program, the embedding of contemporary, and now cognitively familiar modes, into our teaching and the learning in honors. For example, if our memories are challenged to engage more swiftly across a

range of stimuli, through synapses that transgress linear time and geographic space, why persist with organizing knowledge in honors in predominantly historicist ways that suggest memory and, indeed historiography, has not changed?;

- honors service and research choices made up of multi- ontologies and epistemologies rather than driven by a world view grounded largely in versions of national political and economic sovereignty.

Our synaptic world is full of opportunity for all honors educators, were we to embrace just a few of these examples, because the contemporary world provides further tools for exploring what human beings are, what we do, how we do it, and to what ends we exist here on this planet. Nothing could be more clearly core to ideals of an honors education. And yet, we have not fully capitalized on this contemporary condition to develop in an era now able to connect and communicate more so than ever in history to provide an honors education that is embedded with principles of diversity, equity and inclusion not by reference to what appears to be delivered in a course or in a moment of service to the community but in the underpinning of all we do, pedagogically, philosophically and practically.

Conclusion: Achieving Complementarity

"We achieve ourselves by sharing ourselves with others" is surely not so challenging a notion to those who look to achieve "exceptional learning and personal standards".[15] Particularly not in the contemporary synaptic world, and particularly not in light of what we know of how strong relationships, teams and leadership is create. Whether in how we collaborate on campus, or in how we envision the creation and empowerment of teams, whether through attention to models of leadership or in a concerted exploration of types of knowledge and their purpose, an honors college or program based on interdependence can exemplify complementarity. This kind of approach is not one where we are forced to accept, because of no viable alternative, that inequity must paradoxically be a part of a principled college honors college or program. Rather, inequity might be part of prevailing social and economic conditions, or seen in the ways in which we find potential honors students presented to

---

[15] National Collegiate Honors Council, 'Definition of Honors Education' NCHC Board of Directors, https://www.nchchonors.org/uploaded/NCHC_FILES/PDFs/Definition-of-Honors-Education.pdf (2013)

us from secondary education or connected with prejudices whereby differences in race, sexuality, gender or physical ability find individuals and groups marginalized. But it is our role to present an alternative if indeed what we mean by "exceptional" in honors education is not elitist but rather "to be of exceptional quality". Then our distinctiveness, and focus on future reward, and on the rites and rights of celebrating types of achievement, can engage with the "delicate network"[16] of what it means to be human. Such is the meaning and spirit and intention of Ubuntu, and such is the potential of contemporary honors education.

---

[16] Desmond Tutu, https://www.youtube.com/watch?v=0wZtfqZ271w (2013).

CHAPTER FIVE

INCREASING DIVERSITY IN HONORS THROUGH A MENTORING PARTNERSHIP WITH LOCAL TITLE I HIGH SCHOOLS AND BUSINESSES

MARTIN DUPUIS, VANESSA MCRAE AND ZHOLEY MARTINEZ BRANDARIZ

Introduction

This chapter provides a case study of a pilot mentoring program, namely, The Elevation Fellows Program. It is also an analysis of the donor relationship with the community partner supporting the work of college access for underserved, economically disadvantaged high school students. Our experiences developing a local "pipeline" for historically underrepresented students in conjunction with a major business partner have broadened our perspective on how to approach this work. While this chapter is based on the first year of a pilot program, we hope to promote a dialogue on ways of engaging a more diverse student population with the support of the community.

The Elevation Fellows Program was established through a partnership between The Burnett Honors College and Elevation Financial Group. The purpose of the partnership was to develop an on-going college access and success mentoring program with local high schools serving historically underrepresented students. The Elevation Financial Group headquarters is located in Winter Park, Florida. In addition to their work in educational access, the company has a long-standing history of global initiatives focusing on economic development through social entrepreneurship. Elevation Financial Group partners with African and Haitian organizations to train and support "social entrepreneurs who build businesses that tackle social problems, create jobs, and promote the rise of sustainable enterprise."[1]

The Burnett Honors College, located in Orlando, Florida, is one of the thirteen colleges at the University of Central Florida. The Burnett Honors College is the home of approximately two-thousand University Honors students, and it houses the Office of Research and Community Engagement. Some of the programs offered through the Office of Research and Community Engagement are designed to help close the gap between the student diversity in Honors and the university as a whole within the next three years. The University of Central Florida (UCF) recently became a Hispanic Serving Institution, a federal designation that assists universities with at least a 25% Hispanic undergraduate population in supporting first generation, majority low income Hispanic. The Honors College currently has a 17% Hispanic enrollment compared to UCF's 25%. Additionally, the Honors College's Black or African American student population is about 1.7% compared to the university's Black or African American student population of 7.3%. Having racial or ethnic parity between Honors and the university is a worthwhile goal, and developing connections with local Title I schools will help us achieve this objective.

The Elevation Fellows program is designed to match peer mentors from the Honors College with high-achieving students at one of three local Title 1 high schools in Orlando, FL. The Honors students' roles are to act as peer mentors for high-achieving high school students as they pursue their dreams of attending college. So what exactly is peer mentoring and why is it beneficial for college students to serve as peer mentors to a diverse group of high-achieving high school students from disadvantaged backgrounds? Peer mentoring is characterized as the act of mentorship between a mentor and mentee who are close in age. In addition to this age proximity, other characteristics could include a trusting relationship between two young people, where the mentor offers guidance, support, and encouragement aimed at strengthening the competence and character of the mentee. Coles and Blacknall explained mentoring as "a valuable strategy to provide students with the emotional and instrumental support they need to achieve the goal of a college degree."[2] Peer mentors

---

[1]   Elevation Financial Group L.L.C. Last modified 2016. Accessed Feburary 1, 2017. http://elevationfinancialgroup.com/

[2]   Coles, Ann. *The Role of Mentoring in College Access and Success*. Washington, DC: Policy Institute for Higher Education, 2011. Accessed February 1, 2017. http://www.ihep.org/research/publications/role-mentoring-college-access-and-success

are in the unique position to be able to relate to their mentees questions, concerns, and anxieties because they have recently been through many of the same experiences themselves.

Mentoring can take place in two contexts, either as informal mentoring or formal mentoring. For the sake of discussion, this chapter focuses on a formal mentoring program model. Formal mentoring utilizes an approach that is structured and intentional and is usually facilitated by an agency or program with a specific aim. Coles and Blacknall explained that "peer mentoring encompass both one-on-one relationships between an older more experienced peer and a younger peer, as well as small groups of students working with an older peer on a particular goal."[3] They further note, "the sponsoring entity recruits and trains the mentors, matches them with their mentees, and provides support over the duration of the relationship."[4]

Jennifer Engle asserts, "a college education is considered the key to achieving economic success and social mobility in American society."[5] She further explains that "first generation college students face numerous challenges including poor academic preparation to inadequate finances to a lack of support from peers or family members all of which makes it difficult to get into and successfully complete college."[6] Tym, McMillon, Barone, and Webster concur with Engle concerning the difficulties faced by first generation students including a lack of knowledge about applying for college and financial assistance and having more difficulty acclimating themselves to college once they enroll.[7] They explained, "students whose parents did not attend college are more likely than their non-first-generation counterparts to be less academically prepared for college."[8] Engle also notes that research has shown that "first-generation college students generally have lower scores on college entrance examinations

---

[3] Ibid., 2.

[4] Ibid., 3.

[5] Engle, Jennifer. "Postsecondary Access and Success for First-Generation College Students." *American Academic* 3, (2008). https://pdfs.semanticscholar.org/e27f/6b423579e29231e22446c0b7777d7b5946bf. pdf

[6] Ibid., 1.

[7] Tym, Carmen, Robin McMillion, Sandra Barone, and Jeff Webster. *First-Generation College Students: A Literature Review*. Round Rock: Texas Guaranteed Student Loan Corporation, 2004. Accessed February 1, 2017. http://files.eric.ed.gov/fulltext/ED542505.pdf

[8] Ibid.,1.

such as and SAT or ACT."[9] Thus, having peer mentors who have recently gone through the college admission process, including taking the entrance examinations, and who have personally experienced college life would be a great advantage for first generation students. Students from the Honors College serve as mentors assisting their mentees through the process of preparing for college admission exams, reviewing and providing feedback on their personal statements, guiding the students through the Free Application for Federal Aid (FASFA) process, and sharing information about college life. For many of these high school students, having someone available who knows how to navigate through the college readiness process and how to assist them in overcoming the anxieties could be the determining factor as to whether the student chooses to pursue his or her dream of going to college.

According to Balemian and Feng, "more than one-third of 5-17-year-olds in the United States are first-generation students, and the highest rate is among underrepresented minority students."[10] The National Center for Education Statistics (2005) reported:

> First-generation students are more likely to be black or Hispanic and come from low-income backgrounds and only 22% enroll in post-secondary education compared to 40% of students whose parents had some college experience and 36% whose parents completed a bachelor's degree.[11]

Tym et al. observe that "the likelihood of high school students enrolling in postsecondary education is strongly related to their parent's educational background."[12] Peer mentoring programs are designed to pair high school students with college students who can help guide them down the path of successful matriculation into post-secondary education.

Studies reveal there is a strong correlation between peer mentorship and academic performance. Transitioning from high school to

---

[9] Engle, "Postsecondary Access and Success for First-Generation College Students"

[10] Balemian, Kara and Jing Feng. "First Generation Students: College Aspirations, Preparedness and Challenges". Presentation at College Board AP Annual Conference, Las Vegas, NV, July 19, 2013. Accessed February 1, 2017. https://research.collegeboard.org/sites/default/files/publications/2013/8/presentatio n-apac-2013-first-generation-college-aspirations-preparedness-challenges.pdf

[11] Chen, Xianglei and Dennis Carrol. *First-Generation Students in Postsecondary Education: A Look at Their College Transcripts*. Washington, DC: U.S. Department of Education, National Center for Education Statistics, 2005.

[12] Tym, *First-Generation College Students: A Literature Review*

college life and independent living are challenging situations for many young adults.[13] While it can be a struggle even for students who come from affluent backgrounds, one would have to assume that it is even more difficult for first-generation students and students coming from disadvantaged backgrounds. The first year in college comes with many adjustments including "organized learning, time management including study and social schedules, developing new social networks and adjusting to the requirements of university styles of learning and teaching."[14] In this regard, peer mentoring programs have been shown to have positive effects on increasing student success and retention rates. Eby and Rhodes explain that "mentoring promotes self-identity and positive self-image; it contributes to reducing risky behavior and facilitates career and academic development."[15] Data obtained from a longitudinal study conducted by Leidenfrost et al. revealed that "after one year of the study mentees had better average grades and passed more courses than non-mentees."[16]

While there are many studies focused on mentoring programs for high-risk students, there appears to be a gap in the literature for peer mentoring programs focused on preparing high-achieving high school students for college access. The Elevation Fellows program will serve as a model program for future case studies.

Elevation Fellows Mentor Program

Originally focusing on 11th – grade students in one local high school, the Elevation Fellows program has evolved to provide college readiness workshops and materials to all interested high school students in three large, local, underserviced schools. Although this pushed the scale of the program beyond its original design, it influenced the implementation of two major components: The Elevation Fellows program which provides content, workshops, and mentoring for selected students in 9th – 12th grade, and the Elevation Scholars program which provides scholarships to a

---

[13] Leidenfrost, Birgit, Barbara Strassnig, Marlene Schütz, Claus-Christian Carbon, and Alfred Schabmann. "The Impact of Peer Mentoring on Mentee Academic Performance: Is Any Mentoring Style Better than No Mentoring at All?" *International Journal of Teaching and Learning in Higher Education* 26, 1 (2014). http://files.eric.ed.gov/fulltext/EJ1043041.pdf

[14] Ibid.,1.

[15] Eby, Lillian T., Jean E. Rhodes, and Tammy D. Allen. "Definition and Evolution of Mentoring." In *The Blackwell Handbook of Mentoring: A Multiple Perspectives Approach*, 7-20. Malden: Blackwell Publishing, 2007.

[16] Leidenfrost, *The Impact of Peer Mentoring on Mentee Academic Performance.*

limited number of selected 11th – grade students.

This unique design was possible due to the partnership between the University of Central Florida's The Burnett Honors College (TBHC), which directly services the Elevation Fellows programs with staff and mentor involvement, and the Elevation Foundations' financial assistance, which provides funds for the Scholars program and employs a program assistant whose time is divided between TBHC and the Elevation Foundation. This staff member is tasked with recruiting and retaining University of Central Florida (UCF) student mentors, matching them with participating high school students, facilitating these mentoring relationships, and developing a program curriculum that aligns with the program's mission.

Since school-based mentoring is a major component of the Elevation Fellows program, high school administrators provide additional collaboration and support. The school-based mentoring model utilizes the school campus as the primary location and school personnel, such as guidance counselors, initiate student participation in the program.[17]

Leadership and guidance counselors from each participating school serve on the program's advisory committee, which meets monthly for implementation meetings. These monthly implementation meetings allow the program to identify school liaisons who assist in providing student data, meeting space, volunteer authorization and supplies. Dynamic site liaisons aid in garnering program support and attendance through tools such as school notification systems, announcements over the school's public address system, and classroom visits.

Through the school-based liaisons, the Elevation Fellows staff identify potential program participants and mentees known as Fellows. To qualify for the mentorship program, high school students must be at the top of their academic cohort, have a high interest in attending a top university, and agree to complete program assignments. The program requested that school liaisons compile and share a list of students in grades $9-11^{th}$ with grade point averages of 3.0 or higher. Currently, the program only initiates the mentor-mentee relationship for 11th – grade Fellows. However, students in grades $9-10^{th}$ still participate in the Elevation Fellows program through grade-specific program assignments and workshops meant to assist them with the college process. (See Appendix A for charts outlining assignments by grade). The students identified by the

---

[17] Jucovy, Linda. *The ABCs of School-Based Mentoring: Technical Assistance Packet #1.* Washington, DC: Department of Justice, Office of Juvenile Justice and Delinquency Prevention, 2008. Accessed February 1, 2017.
https://eric.ed.gov/?id=ED449433

guidance counselors are invited to a kickoff event where the program staff presents the Elevations Fellows Program and the Elevation Scholars Program. Participating students in the program complete a contact card, a code of conduct, and an honor code.

With the assistance of the identified school liaison, Fellows who complete all the program forms and are in 11th – grade are invited to a mentee orientation session where they are presented with the expectations, roles, and goals for the facilitated mentor relationship. At the end of the Mentee orientation, these students are asked to complete a mentee matching sheet and agreement, which provides the Elevation Fellow's program assistant with the necessary information to initiate the matching process.

Once a pool of interested high school students is recruited, the program assistant begins to identify potential mentors from the University of Central Florida. Mentors are expected to be high-achieving and are often recruited from within TBHC. The Elevation Fellows program follows a public relations plan that was designed to achieve three fundamental priorities: build broad awareness of Elevation Fellows at the university; increase our network of volunteers; and strengthen tools to attract, retain and cultivate individuals committed to advocating on behalf of the Elevation Fellows program. The public relations plan outlines several strategies to increase traditional and social media coverage of the program. These include, but are not limited to:

1. Identify the most compelling stories the organization should tell and showcase those stories in our communication via Honors newsletter, Honors social media websites, and University publications.
2. Outline specific key messages that best tell the organization's story and use those messages to guide all our communication.
3. Identify key university and community resources that regularly showcase education and volunteering to begin building relationships with them.
4. Distribute program flyers during Honors service learning courses and the first week of classes.
5. Request for mentors should be placed in Honors newsletter, university publications, and social media from the first week of classes until the need is met.
6. Provide interest meetings and tabling at the Honors college and university to broadcast program and recruit volunteers.
7. Provide training and certificates for participating mentors.

All recruitment materials include the following: program mission, general eligibility (i.e. grade point averages needed, time commitment expected), partner schools, and benefits of participation. Interested students are always advised to review the program's mentor responsibilities and partner school times before proceeding with the application (See Appendix B for mentor responsibilities).

Eligible mentors are expected to complete an orientation session and a mentor matching sheet. The mentor matching sheet is used during the matching process in conjunction with the completed mentee matching sheets. During the matching process, the mentees' gender, educational and career goals, education area of interest, and personality types are heavily weighed against the potential mentor's responses. In both matching forms, several questions are provided to understand the student's expectations of post-secondary attainment and personality type. We utilize those responses to then identify mentors who are experiencing the post-secondary goals the high-school student would like to achieve. Although not every mentor-mentee relationship can be perfectly coordinated, the education area of interest, and other items such as hobbies and expectations, allow for a common ground to be identified between the mentor-mentee applications in the matching process.

The program assistant initiates the relationship by contacting the mentor and mentee via email with their respective contact information and completed profiles. Mentors are provided a sample message, which includes potential meetings, to assist communication. Matched mentors are also asked to complete registration in the selected schools' volunteer management system. In addition to meeting with their mentees during one-on-one meetings at the school, mentors are also invited to program workshops and events. This encourages group mentoring and higher engagement rates for the mentor and mentee.

Mentor training, support, and follow-up are required after initial matching is completed. The program assistant provides both mentors and mentees with program updates via a newsletter and invites them to join the Elevation Fellows Facebook group. A completed mentoring agreement which provides expectations for the relationship, meeting times, and duration must be turned into the program assistant after the initial meeting (See Appendix C). Volunteer hour submissions, workshops, phone-calls, emails, and volunteer appreciation events are methods the program utilizes to continue engagement with the matched mentor and mentees.

Although the Elevation Fellows program is the major mentoring component of the program our partnership allows eligible Fellows to also participate in the Elevation Scholars program. Through funding provided by the Elevation Foundation the Elevation Scholars program provides financial support to a limited number of selected 11th – grade students planning on attending a post-secondary institution. This incentive encourages many of the 9-10th grade students to continue participation in the Elevation Fellows program until they are eligible for mentoring and potentially rewards them for completion.

Our first two years with the Elevation Foundation and TBHC have illuminated a number of lessons that might be beneficial to other Honors programs considering such a program. First, the program probably does not need to include funding for tuition. Initially, Elevation Financial thought they would fund tuition support. However, the high school students targeted are eligible for need-based and merit scholarships, and with proper advising, will often receive financial support for the entire cost of attendance at a university. There is a need, though, for support in the application process and for spending and travel money once in college. A hallmark of the Elevation Scholars program is also funding for two summer internships, one in community service and one in business.

Second, using social media, developing on-line content, and having group sessions on important topics like the personal statement, resumes, and test preparation was very effective. These "boot camps," open to participating Fellows, not only delivered important content, they also created a support group for these high-achieving high school students. These Saturday morning sessions brought together great students from across the three participating high schools, too. Uber, paid for by Elevation Financial, is used to transport high school students to the workshops. (The high school student has to be over 18 years of age to ride Uber or an adult has to accompany them). The Honors College mentors provided their perspective and helped the high school students write and edit their work. We found it challenging to schedule programs after school because of work or co-curricular activities, but mentors and mentees usually carved out convenient times on their own. Lunch breaks even worked for some teams. Maintaining the connection between mentors and protégés also takes some nurture, but social media provides a convenient platform for young people.

Attracting Donors

Mentoring programs such as the one described provide incredible opportunities for community partnerships and financial support. The Elevation Financial Group, the sponsor of our program, is a prime example. The Elevation Financial Group is a real estate company focusing on purchasing and operating affordable housing complexes. They are so committed to corporate social responsibility that they created the Elevation Foundation with a mission "[t]o transform distressed communities by elevating entrepreneurship and educational opportunity locally and globally through strategic investments that produce measurable results." The Elevation Foundation was already working in a Title I high school when the Burnett Honors College began talking about how we could partner to assist more of these high school students in applying to prestigious universities and to encourage more applications from historically underrepresented students to the Honors college. The Elevation Foundation had been selecting a few of the most outstanding students to receive support in the application process and financial support for travel and summer programs while in college. By collaborating with the Burnett Honors College in a mentoring program, we are able to work with hundreds of additional high school students.

While there are many worthwhile causes, higher education and the impact it has on individuals and communities is one of the most important issues. Educational access is a compelling programmatic area for donors, businesses, Honors programs, and school districts. There is also a natural synergy or alliance for all these community partners in supporting the college application process. Scott Lee, Vice President of Business and Philanthropic Development for Elevation Financial Group, commented, "In the US, education is most significant lever" in addressing inequality.[18] The income difference between high school dropouts and people with a college education is twice as much over a lifetime.[19]

Paul Morgan, one of the principals of Elevation Financial, said they focused their philanthropy on "where they could get the most leverage; where they could be most transformative."[20] The conclusion was education. Their strategy is to "look for kids in Title I schools who had the potential to be national leaders but either didn't know or wouldn't realize it because of their surroundings." In addition, they want to convince people it is worthwhile to create future leaders from diverse backgrounds.

---

[18] Scott Lee (Elevation Financial Group L.L.C.), interviewed by Martin Dupuis, Winter Park, FL, December 15, 2016.
[19] Cahalan, Margaret and Laura Perna. *Indicators of Higher Education Equity in the United States: 45 Year Trend.* Washington, D.C: The Pell Institute, 2015 Revised Edition. http://www.pellinstitute.org/downloads/publications-Indicators _of_Higher_Education_Equity_in_the_US_45_Year_Trend_Report.pdf.
[20] Paul Morgan (Elevation Financial Group L.L.C.), interviewed by Martin Dupuis, The Burnett Honors College, UCF, Orlando, FL, February 1, 2017.

After their first year of developing the program, they realized that they could not just work with seniors because they have missed out on too many opportunities. A successful mentoring program needs to start sooner, in the ninth and tenth grades. Mr. Morgan stated that the goal is to "change aspirations!" Title I students may not have the aspiration to go to elite schools because it never occurred to them or the school counselor that they were capable and able to go. By exposing these Title 1 high school students to other Honors students, we can demonstrate how it is done and inspire them to consider academic goals that may never have even occurred to them.

Given this opportunity to make such a difference in young people's lives, creating a partnership in the community with donor support has great potential. Honors programs are uniquely qualified to provide guidance to inexperienced college applicants since our students have done well on standardized tests, have earned good grades in a rigorous curriculum, have written strong personal essays, and have been leaders in their communities. Honors students are recently minted experts in this area, and they can relate well to the high school students who are just slightly younger in age. While admission criteria will vary by Honors program, Honors students themselves are excellent tutors for college application. They bring their experience and a student perspective to the process.

School districts are often eager to connect with Honors programs, and building bridges between secondary and university systems has benefits for both institutions. Creating a pipeline of students from Title I high schools to the Honors program and university assists with minority recruitment. It also helps ensure that the best local students apply for admission. Developing champions or key influential contact people in the school district and the high schools themselves is very important. Many school systems have minority achievement officers or leadership in the superintendent's office that can make resources available or assist at the school level. Principals, guidance counselors, and the teachers of special program like the International Baccalaureate, Advanced Placement, or Dual Enrollment programs are essential for identifying and recruiting high-achieving high school students as well as securing rooms for events and assisting with logistics.

Donors, businesses and other community stakeholders are additional partners that can elevate the scope and impact of a mentoring program. The potential for making a significant difference in young people's lives and in the community through educational access might appeal to many organizations and individuals willing to contribute to such a program. With the Elevation Financial Group as a case study, the motivation for choosing to partner and effective ways to communicate impact with donors will be explored.

As mentioned, the Elevation Financial Group was already interested in working on college access for underserved students. They had started out by competitively selecting a few of the best high school students and offering them funding for professional college preparatory services, tuition, and summer internship opportunities. They were inspired by meeting extremely talented students in Title I high schools who have incredible leadership potential and want to make a difference in their community. However, these young people might never develop without opportunities to attend great universities. There is the risk that too many of these young people would sell themselves short because they do not have the knowledge of how to apply to schools and for financial aid. Title I high school students may have family issues, financial concerns, lack of experience and little understanding of the university system that impede their ability to enter prestigious universities or Honors colleges.

The leadership of the Elevation Foundation met numerous times with Honors and university staff to discuss the support, opportunities, and services that first generation college applicant's need. Some of the beneficial attributes Honors could bring to this partnership include educational expertise and resources, experience with the college admission process, an understanding of financial aid and the Free Application for Federal Student Aid (FAFSA), and college success strategies for freshmen students. In addition, Honors programs have a cadre of excellent students who can share their first-hand experience, serve as role models, help tutor, and assist with practice SAT or ACT tests. By partnering with the Honors college, the Elevation Foundation is able to expand its reach and impact more high school students. Mr. Lee commented, "The Honors college connects amazingly high performing students, especially those from diverse backgrounds, with the dedication and drive to inspire younger high school students. Honors programs bring expertise and resources, people and programs, to truly partner with the school district and with people who have the financial means to provide the funds to create these programs."

Our experience offers a case study for engaging donors, and there are some valuable insights into their thinking and decision-making. Donors who are currently supporting first-generation or minority achievement scholarships might be persuaded to do more if they can see how their funding of a program will have even greater impact. Current donors and others in the community concerned about these issues could come together to help create the program. The school district and its supporters are also valuable partners. A coalition can accomplish a lot more than individual, disparate work. The Honors program can help be the catalyst that brings it all together! Starting small with one Title I high school is a good start. As these high school students succeed in college, they become the best ambassadors for the program. It is even possible to have a donor adopt a high school program or to name the award package for the recipient after a donor.

The Elevation Financial Group discussed their charitable giving in a very interesting way: as a business decision. It seems that donors are often approached based on the merit or altruistic value of a program, and these are important rationales. The impact of a college education on a Title I high school student will last a lifetime and may even have a generational influence. This is difficult to measure, however.

An additional way of presenting the case focuses on what businesses are most concerned with, return on investment. Mr. Lee, who has years of experience as the director of an international foundation, observes that too often non-profits do not "work, speak, communicate or measure in terms that business people are comfortable with." There is a tendency to measure activity instead of results, with programs celebrating the number of students participating. A more rigorous assessment will focus on the money and resources put in versus the value of the return. Elevation Financial, with their private equity mindset, looks for a ten percent return on their investment. For example, if a program cost $25,000, investors or donors would be impressed with a $250,000 return. The return can be measured monetarily by the financial aid and scholarship funding these high school students receive. This perspective offers a somewhat unique way of evaluating a program, and the rigor of assessment can make a program more attractive to donors.

The Elevation Financial program costs $250,000 a year, so they expect to see the students they work with receive a total of $2.5 million dollars in college support. They use this analysis to attract their investors to also become donors to the program, and three out of four solicited decided to participate. Many investors make investment decisions faster and easier with larger amounts of money than they do with their philanthropic giving. They may quickly be able to choose a $150,000 investment opportunity, but it might take many months to make a $10,000 charitable gift. Philanthropic giving may be outside their comfort zone. They often have certain sums of money set aside for investing, but many people do not have a budget set aside for charitable giving. Helping a donor understand that their philanthropic donation is a good investment can motivate them to participate.

Of course, there are other assessment methods that will attract donors. For Honors programs the number of students matriculating from diverse backgrounds is an important measure. For the program, the number of students attending prestigious schools is impressive to report. The high school students can also comment on the ways in which their academic horizons are expanded. Any improvement in standardized test scores is important. The development of leadership skills for the Honors college student mentors and their sense of belonging to a community can be evaluated.

There is great value in a Title I high school mentoring program for first-generation college students, for the Honors student mentors, and for Honors programs as it reaches out to more diverse students. This value can also be translated for donors as an excellent return on investment. A more diverse Honors student body will help develop skills for deserving students from historically underrepresented groups and will help inform and cultivate better leaders across the university. This type of program can be created on a size and scale that would fit any Honors program and community. We look forward to seeing the impact of these programs on both students and Honors enrollments in the near future.

Appendix A

9th Grade

University of Central Florida

December	January	February	June
Elevation Fellows Kickoff Event	Afford to Dream and Class Rigor Worksheets	High School Resume and Community Service Workshop	Summer Celebration
Provide a program overview to selected fellows and their parents	Topic 1: Afford to Dream Allow students to research top ranked universities and important factors when considering applying for college	Topic 1: High School Resume Provide fellows with the information needed to create a strong high school resume	Plan and execute fun event for Elevation Fellows and families at school first week after school
	Topic 2: Class Rigor Students will develop a clear class schedule for all four years of high school	Topic 2: Community Service Deliver a presentation and provide opportunities pertaining to community service	

University of Central Florida

10th Grade

September	November	December	February	June
Summer Review and My Year Plan	**University Exploration**	**Elevation Fellows Kickoff Event**	**Personality and Career Test**	**Summer Celebration**
Have students send in a report of what they did during the summer and their plan for the upcoming year	Help them explore Florida universities, small liberal arts colleges, and selective universities	Provide a program overview to selected fellows and their parents	Allow Fellows to find career paths that fit their personality, interest, and aspirations.	Plan and execute fun event for Elevation Fellows and families at school first week after school

11th Grade

University of Central Florida

September	November	December	January	February
Summer Review and My Year Plan	**College Admissions Process and Campus Visit**	**Elevation Fellows Kickoff Event**	**Ongoing Standardized Test Preparation**	**Securing Scholarships Presentation**
Have students document their yearly plan and review summer activities	Allow students to visit a college campus and learn how to successfully navigate the college admissions process	Provide a program overview to selected fellows and their parents		Allow students to learn about financing post-secondary education through scholars
ACT/SAT Practice Examination				**Ongoing Standardized Test Preparation**

March	April	May	June	July
Elevation Financial Scholarship Application	**ACT/SAT Practice Examination**	**Elevation Financial Scholarships Awarded**	**Summer Celebration**	**College Admissions Boot Camp**
Ongoing Standardized Test Preparation	**Ongoing Standardized Test Preparation**		Plan and execute fun event for Elevation Fellows and families at school first week after school	Give students the knowledge and training necessary to navigate and complete the college admissions process

12th Grade

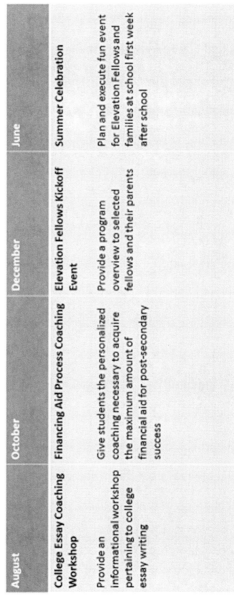

August	October	December	June
College Essay Coaching Workshop	**Financing Aid Process Coaching**	**Elevation Fellows Kickoff Event**	**Summer Celebration**
Provide an informational workshop pertaining to college essay writing	Give students the personalized coaching necessary to acquire the maximum amount of financial aid for post-secondary success	Provide a program overview to selected fellows and their parents	Plan and execute fun event for Elevation Fellows and families at school first week after school

Appendix B

Mentor Responsibilities

Mentors agree to the following when they complete the mentor matching sheet and orientation:

- Serve as role models and academic mentor for high school students participating in the Elevation Fellows Program
- Participate in events that focus on college readiness and success at participating schools
- Sharing how they applied to college and their college experience
- Reading over their mentees college and scholarship essays
- Tracking their mentoring hours
- Inspiring mentees to dream big
- Mentors must meet with their mentees at least once a month
- Mentors are expected to communicate with their mentee through email during their service
- Occasional mentor meetings in The Burnett Honors College may occur
- Commit for the duration of the academic year

Appendix C

Elevation Fellows - Mentoring Agreement

Mentorship Agreement: The purpose of this document is to assist you in detailing mutually agreed upon goals and parameters that will serve as the foundation for your mentoring relationships.

Goals (what you hope to achieve as a result of this relationship; e.g., college admissions information, scholarship information, test preparation, college life, finding your major, senior year, networking)

_____
_____
_____
_____

Meeting Frequency (frequency, duration, and location of meeting):

_____
_____
_____

Tracking All mentorship meetings must be logged. All hours that mentor and mentee meet should be tracked through ORCE's volunteer hours' tracker.

Relationship Closure If either party finds the mentoring relationship unproductive and request that it be terminated, we agree to honor that individual's decision without question or blame. Mentor must contact Elevation Program Assistant if this decision is made.

Duration This mentorship relationship will continue if both parties feel comfortable with its productivity or until:

_____

Mentor's Signature:
Date:
Mentee's Signature:
Date:
Parent/Guardian's Signature:
Date:

CHAPTER SIX

CHALLENGES AND POSSIBLE SOLUTIONS IN MINORITY STUDENT RECRUITMENT IN HONORS PROGRAMS AT RURAL COLLEGES AND UNIVERSITIES

ROD D. RAEHSLER

Introduction

The competition for gifted students qualifying for honors colleges and programs has always been a significant focus for academic leaders. With mission goals of program diversity, the competition for students among racial or cultural minority groups is even more protracted. While this is a universal issue confronted by all honors college deans and program directors, the challenge to achieve greater student diversity in a rural environment faces even greater obstacles. Population changes and limitations in financial resources are two important impediments confronted by smaller programs wishing to provide students in honors education a diverse learning environment. This chapter considers addressing the recruitment challenge from this constrained perspective.

My primary interest in this subject is one born out of necessity. Having served as the honors program director at Clarion University nearly four years following the tenure of a highly successful predecessor, I was given an administrative charge to grow the enrollment among our highly qualified students. In that same timeframe, the Director of Minority Services on campus asked me to explore ways to bring in high-achieving minority students who were falling short of the honors program admission requirements (he had also been tasked with growing the enrollment of minority students on campus). As a consequence, I became familiar with the minority achievement gap literature and the subsequent challenges it has created concerning the admissions process.

While the minority achievement gap does take on a wide range of definitions, the relevance it has to honors education relates to the empirical difference in standardized test scores used for admissions. The most recent statistics on average SAT scores provided by the College Board for high school students show that white students score, on average, 206 points higher than African American students. This gap is relatively higher in mathematics (a gap of 108 points) and is one that has not significantly changed for decades. This creates a challenge among programs that utilize standardized tests for admission if a goal of student diversity is an important mission. In this chapter I will outline some important issues relevant to minority student recruitment into honors colleges and programs in rural environments. I will do this by focusing on issues specific to Clarion University under the assumption that many other similar programs face the same types of challenges. Much of the analysis will focus on completed and ongoing internal studies as well as information provided by other leaders to help determine possible solutions that need to be developed.

Related Literature on Diversity

The achievement of diversity among faculty and students has been a longstanding goal in most academic settings. A joint publication by the American Council on Education and the American Association of University Professors in 2000 published[1] a collection of three research papers designed to study whether diversity made a difference in higher education. The first study by Geoffrey Maruyama and Jose Moreno focused on faculty views about the value of diversity on campus and in the classroom. They analyzed survey responses of 544 faculty members addressing six research questions and found that results supported the claim that diversity enhances learning at large, research-oriented universities. Virtually all faculty members espoused the positive impact of classroom diversity with modestly higher ratings among minority faculty members. They concluded that as the academy becomes more diverse over time, support for greater diversity on campus and in the classroom will expand. Of greatest interest was their view that a major challenge for academic institutions in trying to attract students who exhibit diverse

[1] *Does Diversity Make a Difference? Three Research Studies on   Diversity in College Classrooms*, Washington, D.C.: American Council on Education and American Association of University Professors, (2000).

attributes and perspectives is how to incorporate this into an effective admission process.

The second study by Roxane Harvey Gudeman[2] concentrated on the link in student diversity and the ability of institutions of higher education to successfully meet mission statements. Her analysis of 28 liberal arts colleges and a survey distributed at one with a fairly homogenous student body found that many were not able to meet the goal of attaining diverse environments for students. Interestingly, her conclusion was that a significant reliance on standardized test scores among small, liberal arts colleges served as an impediment in attracting many talented minority students. The third study in the document by Patricia Marin describes the positive educational attributes of a diverse classroom environment. Her primary thesis was that the critical thinking skills of students along with the teaching effectiveness of the instructor is enhanced with diverse classroom populations. A more precise study using longitudinal data sets conducted by Gurin, Dey, Hurtado, and Gurin[3] empirically verified that diverse experiences had robust effects on all important learning outcomes. This included the development of stronger critical thinking skills. Furthermore, they found that diversity achieved in informal settings was more important in the overall learning process than simply having diverse classroom settings. As a consequence, the educational gains from a diverse student population can be enhanced by developing strong student organizations and opportunities that promote diversity. Taken together, these studies imply that there are significant challenges among all academic institutions in attracting minority students. These challenges might be solved by changing admission standards. In any case, the academic advantages in developing a diverse student population in any environment are substantial.

While these results can be translated to honors education recruitment initiatives, it does not appear there was much focus on how to directly promote diversity in an honors environment. One exception is by Anthony Pittman who, in 2001,[4] published an article that first took a look at how honors programs in higher education can be linked to diversity

---

[2] *Does Diversity Make a Difference? Three Research Studies on   Diversity in College Classrooms*, (Washington, D.C.: American Council on Education and American Association of University Professors, (2000).

[3] P. Gurin, E. Dey, S. Hurtado, and G. Gurin "Diversity and Higher Education: Theory and Impact on Educational Outcomes." *Harvard Educational Review* 72, no. 3 (2002): 330-366.

[4] A Pittman, "Diversity Issues and Honors Education." *The National Honors Report* 22, no. 2 (2001): 28-30.

issues. His work presented overall survey results from a very small sample of students in the Honors Program at the University of Connecticut. The study provided some initial insight as to how different students view issues related to diversity. This initial study was developed so that university honors colleges and programs might be able to benefit from the advantages expected from obtaining a more culturally diverse student population; similar to that espoused by the American Council on Education. What Pittman found among students was a distinctly different view concerning diversity issues in their particular program.

Students participating in the survey were asked three very basic questions. They were first asked whether or not they felt that there were any barriers in the program that may prevent a minority student to fully participate in the honors program and to explain their response. The second question asked students to outline any reasons why minority students may be made to feel uncomfortable in participating in the honors program at the University of Connecticut. Finally, students were asked if they believed the honors program prepared them to interact with individuals from other races. Interestingly, nonwhite students reported that barriers to minority student participation related to the existing lack of diversity, misperceptions of the honors program being an elitist organization, and the false belief that honors participation resulted in an unnecessary addition to existing course loads. White students, on the other hand, perceived barriers to exist from a diminished performance on standardized tests for nonwhite students along with lackluster recruiting efforts by the program. It is interesting that nonwhite students tended to focus on the existing characteristics of the program (either actual or perceived) while white students looked more at the admission process. These are essentially two different sides of the admissions market and it would be interesting to see whether the same pattern holds with larger and more varied samples.

In a similar fashion, minority students taking the survey did not believe the honors program was adequately preparing students to interact with individuals from different races while white students taking part in the survey strongly believed the opposite to be true. Despite these differing views and the small sample size of the study, administrators in the Honors Program at the University of Connecticut took notice and began a series of initiatives designed to improve the degree of diversity in the program. These involved the development of a colloquium addressing race and diversity along with an exploration as to how to change admission and recruitment activities to attract minority students. Pittman[5] augmented his discussion by outlining the work in Cook[6] that provided some key recommendations as to how to enhance diversity in an honors college or program environment. These included developing stronger support systems within the program to support minority students, investigating the possibility of providing more scholarships and other forms of financial support for minority students, and to disseminate program information in a method that targets a wide range of minority students applying to universities. These specifically involve direct contact with high schools, the efficient dissemination of recruitment material, and announcements in the media targeting minority student populations. As will be apparent, this advice is relevant to challenges faced today by many honors programs; especially at institutions in rural environments.

Clarion University Honors Program Analysis

In order to develop an academic policy designed to attract minority students to a rural honors program, it is important to gain knowledge from as many sources as possible. This would include the use of student data and perceptions specific to the institution (Clarion University in my case) as well as from other academic leaders facing similar circumstances. This section summarizes a series of empirical studies that have been conducted in order to better understand how the minority achievement gap affects this particular rural program.

Before outlining the various internal studies, it is worth outlining the overall environment of the Honors Program at Clarion University to provide some initial perspective. Clarion is a small, rural town in western Pennsylvania approximately 100 miles northeast of Pittsburgh, Pennsylvania. As with most rural areas, the vast majority of the population is white (94.55% according to the 2010 census statistics) and with average income levels below the national average. The region is politically conservative and the local economy is primarily driven by the university. As would be expected, the population of students is slightly more racially diverse with 84.4 percent white and approximately eight percent African-

---

[5] A Pittman, "Diversity Issues and Honors Education." *The National Honors Report* 22, no. 2 (2001): 28-30.
[6] R. Cook, "An Examination of Issues Affecting African American Students' Decisions to Enroll in Honors Programs or Honors Colleges at Predominantly White Postsecondary Institutions", Ph.D. diss., University of South Carolina, (1999).

American. The remaining students are either other races, multiracial, or were unwilling to provide this demographic information.

Raehsler[7] presents results from a survey distributed to students in the honors program on campus in the spring semester of 2016. The survey looked at student responses on questions related to the minority achievement gap and to provide thoughts on how to improve program diversity. The aggregate survey results of the student sample shows that there was significant agreement that standardized testing contributes to the minority achievement gap because it does not accurately measure what students know and what they can do. On average there was also agreement with the notion that a lower proportion of minority students are admitted to honors colleges and programs and that it is a significant problem facing colleges and universities today. Therefore, the average honors student, even in this particular rural setting, seems to have a sense that a problem exists and that it does affect admission at a concerning level. Interestingly, the same students did not generally provide clarity with regard to the possible solutions facing any honors college or program with regards to this achievement gap. Students clearly did not believe the admission standard for the program should be altered to adjust for the SAT gap in scores but, at the same time, were generally neutral when it came to suggesting that better recruitment efforts are needed to boost minority enrollment. The recognition of the problem without a clear solution is perplexing. On the remaining questions that explored perceived reasons for the minority achievement gap, students in the sample were generally in agreement that the location of the high school (urban, suburban, or rural settings), socioeconomic factors, peer pressure from friends, historical segregation, a lack of access to quality schools, and the level of parental involvement were all contributing factors to the achievement gap among minority students. These are consistent with results of similar studies.

Differences seen across students with varying characteristics in the sample with regard to their perceptions on each question are interesting. On the question indicating the degree of knowledge on the issues related to the minority achievement gap, those that provided highly inflated estimates as to the SAT differential also felt less informed. Those that believed they were better informed, as well as those who tended to agree that the minority achievement gap affects admission into the honors program, tended to also agree that the minority achievement gap translates to a gap in academic performance in honors courses. Students who were

---

[7] R. Raehsler, "An Empirical Analysis of Academic Achievement Among Minority Honors Program Students." *Working Paper 201501*, Clarion University Honors Program, (2015).

more advanced in the honors program and those with higher overall grade point averages tended to agree with the claim that the minority achievement gap affects admission rates between races. Interestingly, minority students in the honors program taking the survey were less apt to agree with this assessment. It would be interesting to further understand this difference in perception and might be something to look at in future research. Minority students in the program do agree, however, that flaws in standardized testing in elementary and secondary schools do lead to a persistence of the minority achievement gap. Likewise, more informed students, students not majoring in a natural science, and those that believe the minority gap influences honors admission all agree with this assessment to a significant degree.

Views on possible solutions to how the minority achievement gap may affect program admission are also varied. All groups within the overall sample disagree with the notion that admission standards using the SAT score should be changed to accommodate this difference (although minority students are neutral on this proposal) but, those who disagree most are among those who are most informed, students with higher overall grade point averages, and students not in the natural sciences. Minority students, students not majoring in a natural science, and those that more strongly believe the minority achievement gap affects admission rates are more likely to agree that better recruitment efforts are needed to correct the problem. Students with higher grade point averages, however, are more inclined to disagree with devoting resources toward better recruitment efforts of minority students. It is interesting, for the most part, that students generally recognize the minority achievement gap as a problem but are reticent to suggest that either changes in recruitment or changes in the admission standards should be undertaken. Students with higher grade point averages are actually opposed to both initiatives since they tended to not believe that the minority achievement gap was a significant problem. Minority students strongly agreed with the conjecture that the minority achievement gap is a major problem in honors programs and were against changes in admission standards but strongly in support of recruitment initiatives.

The perceptions with regard to possible causes for the minority achievement gap follow some important patterns across student groups in the survey as well. Minority student in the Honors Program more strongly agreed that historical segregation along with the location of school and lower socioeconomic status among minority families have significantly impacted the minority achievement gap. This same group, interestingly, tended to disagree more with the notion that the lack of access to quality schools or a lack of effort among minority students could be used to explain the persistence of this gap. Among students in the sample who believe the minority achievement gap leads to differences in admission rates in honors colleges and programs there is significant agreement that historical segregation, the location of schools, and the lack of access to quality schools are important factors causing the gap. This group also slightly agrees more that negative peer pressure is also a contributing factor. Students that were either well-informed about the minority achievement gap or not majoring in a natural science were more likely to place a higher weight on the choice of quality schools, socioeconomic status, and teacher expectations on perpetuating the minority achievement gap among high school students. The vast majority of these students either majored in a social science or in education. As a consequence, it is not surprising that this group would focus on institutional educational issues. This may help explain the confusing result that students generally do not support changing admission standards or placing more resources in recruitment efforts. My experience is that students in education will be more likely to view policies that change existing educational institutions as the best way to solve how the minority achievement gap influences honors college or program admission of minority students. It is clear from the survey, however, that there is a wide variety of views and perceptions among students with regard to this issue. Rather than relying solely on student perceptions, a more informative avenue may be to ask current honors education leaders for advice.

Raehsler[8] presents results of a survey sent to all academic leaders of honors colleges and programs in the United States posing similar questions given to the Clarion University Honors Program students. There were a total of sixty responses in the survey that was provided with logistical support from the National Collegiate Honors Council. Of those that responded, a little more than thirteen percent were deans of honors colleges with the remainder serving as directors of programs or colleges. The majority of leaders responding represented programs that had fewer than 300 students (approximately 63 percent of responses). Three-fourths of those responding represented four-year public or private institutions and ninety percent either emphasized teaching or gave teaching an equal footing to research when evaluating faculty performance. Slightly over half of the respondents were female and 91.67 percent were Caucasian. Overall student populations of the programs or colleges represented by

---

[8] R. Raehsler, "Survey of Honors College and Program Leaders on the Minority Achievement Gap." *Working Paper 201602,* Clarion University Honors Program, (2016).

those responding were much more diverse. Approximately two-thirds of students in the respondent programs were white while black and Hispanic students in honors were each at thirteen percent.

The survey results of program directors or college deans, particularly in comparison to student responses in the Clarion University program, are very interesting. For the most part, perceptions of deans and directors display much less variability as these leaders seemed much more decisive with their opinions. There is very strong agreement, for example, that the minority achievement gap is a significant problem facing universities and honors education. While the student survey showed some indecisiveness with regard to possible solutions to the problem, this was not seen among academic leaders. Honors deans and directors strongly favored the approach to heavily recruit minority students as a solution but were in strong disagreement that empirical admission standards needed to be changed in order to adjust for the SAT gap. This is not to say admission standards need not be changed, but that numerical standards should not be altered in an ad hoc fashion. The emphasis on recruitment is important in that it combines different agencies in any university setting.

It is worth noting that honors college or program leaders that responded to the survey viewed themselves as being well-informed about the minority achievement gap and believe, in general, that it does lead to a lower proportion of minority students being admitted into honors colleges and programs. Respondents also strongly believed that the minority achievement gap has been perpetuated by the emphasis on standardized testing in elementary and secondary school settings. Interestingly, the average response was neutral on the question as to whether the minority achievement gap affects later academic performance. Respondents in the honors dean and director survey were also very decisive when asked about factors causing the minority achievement gap over time. On average, there was agreement that each of the following factors were very important causes of the minority achievement gap (listed from most important to least):

- Socioeconomic status and access to quality schools (both tied for greatest agreement)
- Location of schools (urban, suburban, or rural)
- Negative peer pressure
- Teacher expectations

While all five factors above were deemed to be important, there was significant agreement that a lack of effort among minority students was not a factor leading to the achievement gap. These results, together, indicate that academic leaders of honors programs view the solution to be somewhat of a dichotomy. It is possible for colleges and programs to enact policies (especially in the form of recruitment initiatives) to counteract the impact of the minority achievement gap on the admission of minority students, but the true, long-term solution likely lies in changing the underlying causes of the gap. This would encompass large-scale changes in economic and educational policy.

Perhaps the most enlightening information provided by the survey of honors college or program administrators came in the advice many gave to try and increase minority student admission in honors. Of the sixty respondents, forty provided some feedback on what programs can do to improve with regard to student diversity. Some emphasis on recruitment was included in 42.5 percent of those providing feedback. The form of recruitment in the advice varied from direct involvement and control by university admission staff to the use of students and leaders going to high schools to speak with gifted students. Some areas of recruitment focused on faculty assigned to courses and work with university student organizations all meant to increase the visibility of the program. One interesting bit of advice was provided by an honors program director at a historically black college and university (HCBU). While that institution does not face issues related to the recruitment of minority students into the honors program, that director pointed out that it is important to first create a program that has a welcoming and family type of atmosphere and to then develop an admission strategy that provides as much flexibility as possible. Once this identity is established, it can be used to proactively recruit minority students.

Thirty percent of those responding focused on the honors program structure and curricular offerings as a way to bring in more minority students. Suggestions included developing courses that incorporate discussions of diversity, assignment of a diverse faculty to courses offered, and the development of a mentoring program designed to promote diversity. A few directors also advised the development of a tutoring program within honors to help those coming in with lower standardized scores assistance in some basic or remedial subjects. Other directors explained that an honors program also needs to be sensitive to the nonacademic needs of students in order to develop a more diverse student body. The program at Clarion University does have a few established student organizations to help create an inclusive atmosphere but we have not explored the idea of tutoring for students in the program. I find this bit of advice to be intriguing as a way to help eliminate any learning gaps that may exist among entering freshmen irrespective of race issues and as a possible recruitment tool.

One-fourth of all responses advised changes to the admission process as a way to bring in minority students. Many directors suggested that admission should be attained through multiple entry points and that the admission process should be more holistic as opposed to relying only on grades and SAT scores. Even though no suggestions were specifically made indicating that a lower numerical standard for admission should be used for minority students, a good number of leaders indicated that over-reliance on standardized score numbers runs counter to adding diversity to any program. Many also specifically pointed out that writing ability and high school class rank appeared to be better predictors of future academic success. This has been confirmed in the Clarion University program through the analysis of historical data. Fifteen percent of those responding advised that increases in scholarships and other funding offers directed toward minority students would be an important addition to any honors college or program strategy to increase student diversity. Budgetary constraints often limit the ability of honors programs to follow this advice, but most admission offices point to financial assistance as the most important tool in attracting students. In most institutions in a rural environment, unfortunately, there is a greater emphasis on attracting a wide variety of students rather than focusing just on honors education. As a consequence, it is difficult to find the funding to devote more scholarship money to minority students even though this appears to be a highly effective solution. The strategic choice taken by many college and university admissions offices to target median students presents an important impediment in recruiting minority students qualifying for honors education among smaller, rural programs. This seems to competitively favor larger and more lucrative urban programs.

The remaining comments made by honors college and program leaders either indicated that their campuses were not experiencing any difficulties in attaining a diverse student body (only five percent of the respondents) or that, despite seeing problems, the advice was that admission should not be based on race but that students should be admitted solely on academic credentials (only another five percent). Even more interesting is that almost forty percent of respondents either indicated that they did not have any advice on how to address the problem in recruiting minority students or simply did not answer the question. Over half of this group requested the results of my study once it was completed. In one respect, this means the difficulty in attracting minority students into honors programs is widespread. With over half of this sample coming from smaller programs in rural settings, it appears this is a more daunting problem for schools in this environment.

Prior internal research that has relevance to issues linked to minority student recruitment appears in Savage, Raehsler, and Fiedor.[9] That paper studied the impact of a wide variety of academic characteristics in order to produce a model to predict whether or not an admitted student would likely complete the Honors Program at Clarion University. Using two decades worth of data, it was found that the only significant variable helping predict completion in the program was the high school grade point average. Interestingly, the standardized test scores used in admission decisions were not statistically significant. This seems to indicate that a change in admissions standards or a move to a more holistic approach as advised by many other deans and directors in the previously discussed survey has some empirical support. This also loosely implies that changing the standardized test requirements to account for gaps among minority students might not adversely affect program completion rates. In order to test this in a comprehensive fashion, I studied the academic performance of all students attending Clarion University from 1990 through 2015 to see how various demographic and academic indicators could help explain overall grades and completion rates. In that study I developed a probit model designed to predict completion rates of students based on various measurable characteristics. In agreement with Savage, Raehsler, and Fiedor,[10] it was found that high school grade point average was a significant predictor of student completion rates while SAT scores did not have a significant impact. Using this model and historical data, I ran a simulation to see how changing admission standards would influence the completion rates of minority students on the Clarion University campus. Using our current high school grade point average and SAT admission criteria, I found that the completion rate for African American students in the sample stood at 42.86 percent. This may seem relatively low, but a portion of those not finishing at Clarion University left for another university by choice. This, unfortunately, cannot be quantified so remains as an incomplete measure in this study. By decreasing the SAT requirement by 100 points, the completion rate only falls to forty percent. Decreasing the SAT admission cutoff by 200 points (the approximate

---

[9] H. Savage., R. Raehsler, and J. Fiedor, "An Empirical Analysis of Factors Affecting Honors Program Completion Rates." *Journal of the National Collegiate Honors Council 15*, no. 1 (2014), 115-128.

[10] Savage, H., Raehsler, R., and Fiedor, J. "An Empirical Analysis of Factors Affecting Honors Program Completion Rates." *Journal of the National Collegiate Honors Council 15*, no. 1 (2014), 115-128.

minority achievement gap) sees the completion rate fall to 33.33 percent; a total drop of only 9.53 percent. Using the high school grade point average, every drop of 0.1 results in a decrease of 4.465 percent in completion rate. Therefore, dropping the high school grade point average requirement by 0.4 would result in a completion rate of 25 percent in the simulation; a much more significant decline. As a consequence, using historical data it appears relaxing the SAT requirement would not have a dramatic impact on student success and represents a possible avenue to bring in high-achieving minority students. While Raehsler[11] is still in a working paper form, current results suggest that a change in admission criteria is in order.

Conclusion

Due to the lack of direct access to a diverse collection of students under a significant degree of institutional barriers, it seems clear that honors programs in rural environments need a multi-pronged approach in order to attract academically gifted minority students. Through the use of a survey of current honors education leaders, a survey of students in the program at Clarion University, and analyses of student completion data it appears that there are a number of possible avenues leaders in honors education might take. These include:

1. An effort to improve the diversity of instructors and material provided in honors courses. An effort to change the curriculum in order to capitalize on existing university strengths.
2. A concerted effort along with admissions offices to reach out to urban locations where a more diverse student population exists. The development of a more active recruitment strategy.
3. The development of a broader, more inclusive program admission policy that moves away from rigid standards and provides opportunities for a wide variety of students.
4. An increase in funding to support student scholarship and research in an honor4s education setting.
5. The establishment and fostering of student organizations that promote diversity in a social setting and help make a program more like a family. Providing academic and social assistance to freshman through these organizations is essential.

---

[11] R. Raehsler, "Survey of Honors College and Program Leaders on the Minority Achievement Gap", *Working Paper 201602*, Clarion University Honors Program, (2016).

As a director of an honors program in a rural environment, I have a great deal of work ahead!

CHAPTER SEVEN

DIVERSIFYING HONORS: A CASE STUDY FROM FERRIS STATE UNIVERSITY HONORS PROGRAM

PETER BRADLEY. JORDAN DAWKINS, MELANIE TRINH, CINDY TRAN AND CAITLYN TOERING

The Problem

The Honors Program at Ferris State university is turning 20 years old in 2017. The first cohort of 81 first-time-in-any-college (hereafter FTIAC) students was admitted in 1997. An additional 51 continuing students in their second or third year of undergraduate work joined the program.

For most of its history, the Program was not a very diverse place. While we do not have demographic data for the first four cohorts, we do have data on the pools of applicants starting with cohort 2001, enrolled students starting in 2010, and the complete admission process starting in 2014. Cohort 2014 marked the first cohort recruited under a new admissions framework, which was put in place by Dr. Bradley upon his arrival to Ferris in January 2013.

In spring 2016, Dr. Bradley pulled together a small working group of Honors students to review these datasets and make recommendations about how we can better appeal to minority students. We found that (a) while changing the admissions threshold to a more inclusive framework in 2013 greatly enhanced the diversity of the program; and (b) there is still a significant loss of prospective African-American students at each step of the admissions process. We investigated (b) further, but were unable to produce any reliable findings. We speculate that there may be some cognitive effects—perhaps imposter syndrome—that disproportionately impact the African-American student, and streamlining the admissions process may be more effective in recruiting from this community.

Context at Ferris State

Ferris State University is a career-focused public university in rural Michigan.

The challenges of recruiting a diverse cohort of students are great: while Michigan is a large, diverse state, Ferris State is in the north-central region, which is one of the poorest regions. To make matters worse, we are just 43 miles from Central Michigan, which is close to twice our size. Our setting is distinctly rural, yet not far enough north to be identified with the outdoors recreational activities promoted by institutions like Northern Michigan University or Michigan Technological University.

The community around Ferris is overwhelming white, poor and rural. According to the 2010 national census, Mecosta County is 93.7% White, with a median household income of $41,889 and 21.3% poverty.[1] Osceola and Lake counties, which are neighbors to the North and Northeast respectively, are frequently in the bottom five counties by household income in Michigan.

We are far enough from the population centers to preclude mass commuting, our location is not distinctive enough to use as a draw, as Northern Michigan's location can be for them. We are far too rural to attract urban populations, and our community is not diverse enough to be attractive to students of color.

Despite these challenges, Ferris has thrived by promoting its distinctive 'career-focused' curriculum. Ferris has a full general education curriculum, complete with distribution requirements and outcomes; yet it arranges its majors as 4-year lock-step tracks with specific careers in mind: pre-pharmacy, pre-optometry, plastics engineering technology, pre-nursing and nursing, etc.

This approach clearly resonates with the expectations of higher education today. Ferris's enrollment—during a demographic and economic downturn in the state—has steadily increased from 9,468 in 1997 to 14,715 in 2015: an average increase of about 9% annually. The state of Michigan suffered the most during the 'Great Recession of 2008', which actually started in 2006 in Michigan. Unemployment rose from 6.8% in Jan 2006 to a peak of 14.9% in Jan 2009. It took until August of

---

[1] Data from the 2010 US Census, accessed via uscensus.gov

2014 for it to dip back below 6.8%.[2] Yet Ferris' distinctive career-focused programs allowed it to grow by 2,000 students during that same period.

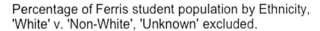

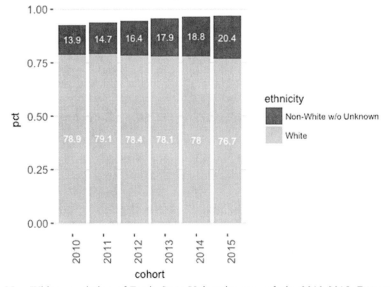

Non-White population of Ferris State University as a whole, 2010-2015. Dataset excludes those who did not respond to the question ('unknown' ethnicity')

This growth has been complemented by a significant increase in the non-white population: from 12% in 2006 to 20% in 2015. Again, given the location and the demographic background of the community we inhabit, this is remarkable.

When viewed on this scale, Ferris is a much more diverse, robust and stable institution than it once was. And for that, it certainly should be lauded. But history is hard to shake off. And the reputations of institutions—and communities—as catering to one type of student or another, can be maddeningly difficult to counter.

---

[2] Data from the US Department of Labor, Bureau of Labor Statistics. Accessed from https://www.bls.gov/eag/

Honors population versus Ferris population

Ferris State went through a significant and sudden decline in enrollment, dropping from a peak of 12,461 in 1992 to 9,468 in 1997.[3] The Honors Program was founded in 1997 in response to this decline—at the lowest point of a decade of enrollment below capacity. As a result, the focus of the Honors Program was to attract and retain students to Ferris. It began as a 'cohort' model live-learn community designed for FTIACs with lock-step progress through a set curriculum, which was consistent with the University's curriculum practices.

With excess residential capacity, the University provided these students a single room at no additional charge throughout their undergraduate career.

Admissions criteria were set at a minimum of 3.4 high-school GPA and a minimum of 24 on the ACT composite. An essay competition, called the 'Invitational,' was created for incoming first-year students, and a minimum score of '2' was determined by faculty in the Languages and Literature department. All admissions criteria were used as minima, whereby a student who met all three minima was accepted, and a student who failed to meet any one, even with strengths in the other two, was not.

The program was primarily focused on preparing undergraduate students for graduate training in our two graduate colleges: The College of Pharmacy and The Michigan College of Optometry. The Program included other majors in the early days but it was, like the pre-pharm and pre-opt, almost entirely white.[4] Between 2002 and 2006, the entering cohort of first-time in any college students varied between 96% and 98% white.

Given the restrictions on the curriculum of students in the lock-step majors pre-professional majors, the Honors Program developed primarily as a co-curricular structure. Students completed 15 hours of community service, which they often organized independently, attended three cultural events per semester and held a formal leadership position in a Registered Student Organization by their fourth year.

Due to lack of emphasis on the curriculum, and its lack of visible diversity, the program was sometimes viewed by faculty and staff as a kind of back-door segregation. This caused, as you might imagine, tension

---

[3] Data originates in Ferris State Factbooks, available for public review at http://www.ferris.edu/HTMLS/admision/testing/factbook/homepage.htm

[4] It is worth noting, then, that neither of these majors, nor professions, is particularly diverse. In fact, the College of Pharmacy fall 2015 reports 84% White (excluding unknown) and the Michigan College of Optometry 87%. This is comparable to Honors' 89% White on the same measure.

between the program and various other offices on campus. When Dr. David Pilgrim, a Sociology professor who taught some of the first Honors classes, was named Associate Vice President for Diversity and Inclusion in 2006, his five-point plan included 'diversify the honors program.' There were a number of administrative attempts to do just that, but none were successful.

In 2013, the founding coordinator of the program retired, and Dr. Bradley (an author) was hired as the new Director. His first major task was to change the admissions requirements to include a modified version of William Sedlacek's non-cognitive questionnaire, which would measure the student's commitment to service and leadership—important parts of the program's mission. At the same time, the minimum ACT and High School GPA required were raised and combined before they were reviewed. Admissions decisions were therefore made on a review of the complete application. Prior to 2014, students were admitted to the program automatically if and only if they had high school GPA over 3.4, ACT over 24 and an essay score greater than 2. Starting in 2014, students who lacked one or two scores over the minimum would be considered if their application showed significant commitment to service and leadership.

While this policy was not intended to diversify the incoming class, but rather to align admissions requirements with the program's purpose statement, it has resulted in three consecutive first-year classes with greater than 10% non-white population. In the 13 years prior to 2014, the program passed that mark only once: 89.9% white in 2011. Semesters are designated by the four digit year and the two-digit numeric month in which the semester began, so '201608' means the semester that started in August 2016, or "Fall 2016."

Ethnic Distribution of all Honors students, W and U remov

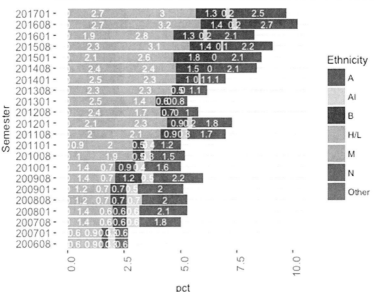

pct

But impediments still remain. As incoming Honors cohorts are still not as diverse as the pool of eligible students, there must be some factor that differentially affects students of different ethnicities in the process of becoming an Honors student.

Honors recruiting versus ethnic distribution of the state

Before we began investigating the recruiting processes of Honors, we wanted to ensure that the recruiting practices of the institution as a whole was not an unseen impediment. The Honors Program only contacts students once they have been accepted to Ferris, and hence, why we judge our success or failure at diversifying the Honors student population against the pool of Ferris State admits who are eligible for Honors—and not the general population of our recruiting areas.

However, if the admitted population of Ferris skewed away from the demographics of the recruiting areas, we might be able to find potential markets. By using data from the 2010 census, we checked the demographic distribution by ethnicity of the 'eligible' Honors student pool against the census data by zip code.

There is no correlation (-0.0037) between the percentage of white residents in a zip code and the total number of students eligible for Honors from that zip code. The distribution of zip codes from which we have at least one student in the eligible pool for Fall 2014-Fall 2016 looks like this:

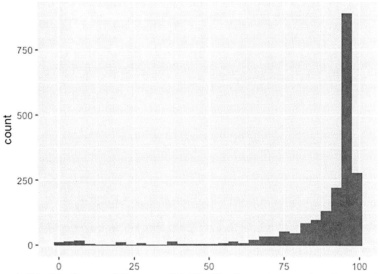

Histogram of eligible students' zip codes by percentage

Our top ten recruiting zips codes, compared to the state's average distribution by ethnicity:

Ethnicity	Top ten Honors recruiting counties	Michigan average
Total population - Hispanic or Latino (H/L)	5.3	3.2
Total population - One Race - American Indian and Alaska Native (AI)	0.7	1.1
Total population - One Race – Asian (A)	1.6	1.1
Total population - One Race - Black or African American (B)	2.7	6.2

Total population - One Race - Native Hawaiian and Other Pacific Islander (N)	0.0	0.0
Total population - One Race – White (W)	91.0	88.6
Total population - Two or More Races (M)	2.0	1.9

The counties where Ferris Honors recruits successfully are *slightly* less diverse than the state, especially in respect to zip codes with a high African-American population. We do have a higher percentage of Hispanic / Latino population in our recruiting areas than the state, however. Our starting population (i.e. 'eligible honors students') is skewed away from serving the African-American population. This may be the result of our rural location, but I do not have data regarding the degree of urbanization by zip code in the existing dataset to establish that fact.

The Honors Application Process

'Eligibility' for Honors, starting in 2014, is defined as having either a minimum of 3.5 high school GPA or a minimum ACT of 25 and having been accepted by Ferris.

Once 'eligible', the student must complete an Honors application. Prior to 2014, the application collected only biographical information. After 2014, it included questions about service and leadership, as well as goals the students has for himself or herself, the students' ultimate educational aspirations and accomplishments of which the student is proud. Students who complete this application are called 'applied.'

Students are then invited to complete the essay. These are 'invited'. Those who complete the essay are then 'accepted', 'rejected' or 'wait-listed.' The final step in the process is for the student to 'confirm' his or her acceptance to the program, thus ensuring priority registration before orientation.

Most students complete the essay on the last Saturday in February at a Campus event we call the 'Invitational.' Students who miss that date, or cannot make the journey (such as out-of-state students) are able to complete the essay at home through a guidance counselor or another responsible adult. These students are classified in our system as 'late admits'.

The entire process takes 8 steps:

1. Apply to Ferris
2. Meet eligibility criteria ('Eligible')
3. Apply to Honors ('Applied')
4. Be invited to take the essay ('Invited')
5. RSVP for the essay ('RSVPYes')
6. Complete the essay ('Complete')
7. Be accepted ('Accepted')
8. Confirm coming ('Confirmed')

The admissions process is a conversation between student and the Honors office. The office takes certain actions (inviting, accepting) and the students take certain actions (applying, completing the essay, confirming). In order to better understand the continuing imbalance in ethnic diversity, I developed a system to look at the relative distribution of students by ethnicity at each step of the admissions process.[5]

The charts included show the results by ethnicity for incoming cohorts 2014, 2015 and 2016.

---

[5] 'Ethnicity' here is limited by the University's data--we have no category for people from the middle-east, people from the Indian subcontinent, for those whose ethnicity is tied to religion (such as 'Jewish'), and unlike the US census, 'Hispanic/Latino' is considered a mutually-exclusive ethnicity like 'African-American' or 'White.' 'International' is also considered an ethnicity, for reasons we do not claim to understand.

Ethnic distribution by admissions process 201608

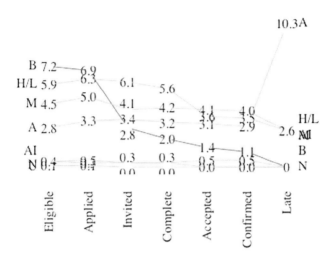

Ethnic distribution by admissions process 201508

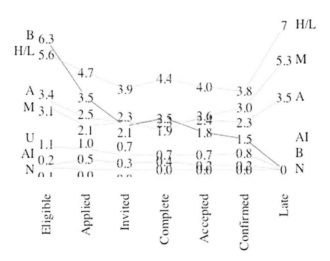

Ethnic distribution by admissions process 201408

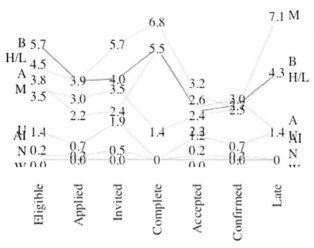

For most ethnic groupings, the proportion of students at each of the steps of the process are equal—the lines are roughly horizontal moving from 'eligible' to 'confirmed.' This is not true for 'Black or African-American' (B).

When we attend solely to the actions completed by the Honors program office, we, thankfully, see no effect of bias, but when we attend solely to the actions of the students, we can see an effect: the net total change across the process, in term of percentage of the previous pool, is contained in the table below. A net of '0' would indicate no change in the percentage of the pool responding with that ethnicity through that stage of admissions.

Ethnicity	Honors Office's decision	Individual's Decision
Asian	-2.88%	0.79%
Black or African American	-1.05%	-4.16%
Hispanic or Latino	-1.11%	-1.06%
Multiracial	2.40%	-2.96%
Native Hawaiian-Pacific Islander	0.00%	0.02%
White	0.38%	10.58%

White students, on average, are making their individual decisions about enrolling in the Honors program differently than their minority-population peers. The difference is the most pronounced when compared to African-American students, who are negative in the individual decisions for all three years sampled.[6] Why is this and what can be done to improve these differences?

Possible confounds

We might think that there are other confounding variables at work here. We can run the same analysis for First Generation status and State of origin. Each of these are single bi-value variables,[7] so we represent different cohorts as data series on the parallel coordinate charts.

First Generation status by admissions process

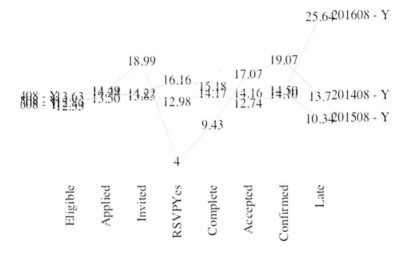

_____

[6] One could note that the negative pattern extends to the 'Multiracial' category in 2014 and 2015, but not 2016. It is hard to say exactly what to make of this, as 'multiracial' could include a huge variety of personal experiences with ethnicity in the US.

[7] We do, actually, allow students to report gender as 'prefer not to say.' The number who do so are statistically insignificant herein, so that response is suppressed in these charts.

State of origin distribution by admissions process

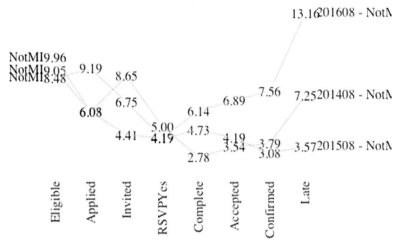

Neither variable appears to explain the differential pattern observed previously.

Students' Exploration

Given that this pattern appears to be robust, we convened a working group of current Honors students and the Director in Spring 2016 to investigate what aspects of our program, marketing or admissions process might differentially attract or repulse students from historically underrepresented populations.

To begin, we identified a number of asked current Ferris students who were eligible for, but did not join, Honors why they didn't apply for Honors. We asked them why. Some of reasons given were:

- Didn't know about the program
- Didn't see themselves as "Honors" students
- Application essay
- Community service requirements

The students determined that they would investigate three areas, in order to determine if there was any language or process requirements that were differentially discouraging minority students from applying.

First, and most importantly, was: How are prospective students learning about Honors? Second, is Honors collaborating with other departments on campus that serve underrepresented groups? Third, are there any psychological factors that may discourage minority students from completing the application process?

How do students learn about Honors?

The students designed a survey to administer on our campus—both to current Honors students and non-Honors students—to gauge what was attractive or problematic in their experience with Honors. We were primarily interested in determining any differences in how the program is perceived by those who joined versus those who chose **not** to join. Unfortunately, the number of respondents who chose **not** to join Honors is very small, and we are unable to draw generalizations out of this dataset. We followed up with some 1-1 interviews with those who did not take the survey. These results are anecdotal, but can provide avenues for future work.

The group found three things: First, that the vast majority of current Honors students learned about the Honors program from our efforts with marketing and recruiting materials. They are not, generally speaking, coming to Honors through the Admissions recruiters. Those who do come to us from recommendations on campus are getting those recommendations from academic advisors, not Admissions or Enrollment Management.

Second, our population appears to underrepresent urban areas in Michigan. We recruit very well in the suburban school districts, but poorly in the urban districts of the same region. This may be consistent with the findings that our top recruiting areas have a smaller African American population than the state as a whole. We have, thus far, been unable to determine why. In fact, we have been unable to determine if this is a cause or an effect of the lack of diversity in Honors.

Third, the 'external benefits' of Honors, rather than the 'internal', appear to be the motivating factor in joining—in particular, many students spoke of the help that Honors provides in getting into graduate or professional school after undergrad. This corresponds to our own preliminary internal findings, that those who aspire to more than a

Bachelor's degree retain to Honors and to Ferris at a higher rate than those who do aspire just to a Bachelor's.[8]

The finding that surprised us most was the fact that most students find out about Honors from Honors marketing material, rather than through admissions. The Ferris Honors Program has long been closely associated with our Pre-Pharmacy and Pre-Optometry programs. These two programs yield enrolled students from the eligible pool at a rate of 28.9% compared to 11% for all other programs combined. We suspect that many of the personal referrals we receive are from those connected to these two programs, or that there is such an association between those who express interest in these programs and Honors that guidance counselors are mentioning Honors to prospective students in these programs, but not in others. Word-of-mouth marketing is notoriously open to subconscious bias and may well be the culprit here.

138 students participated in our survey. They were recruited by the Honors program using its standard messaging system (blog, Twitter, Facebook and email), as well as through direct contact by the students conducting the survey. The survey was presented to minority-serving registered student organizations in an attempt to raise the number of non-Honors student participants. While the personal touch worked as a reminder for the Honors students participating in these RSOs, raising the number of Honors student participants, it did little to raise the number of non-Honors student participants.

We asked the students: "With which ethnicity do you most identify (using the categories used by Ferris):" The results are presented below:

---

[8] The Honors Application at Ferris asks the question: "What is your total lifetime expected education?" The dataset is limited somewhat as we've only asked this question since 2014, and retention rates for that cohort are only becoming clear now, in 2017. But, since 2014, the average number of semesters completed in Honors for students anticipating only a Bachelor's is 2.2 compared with 2.4 for those anticipating some form of graduate school. The effect is slightly more pronounced in retention to Ferris, where the average number of semesters completed is 2.4 of those expecting bachelor compared with 2.7 for those anticipating graduate school.

Ethnicity	Freq	pct
AI	1	0.7
A	7	5.1
B	3	2.2
H/L	2	1.4
M	1	0.7
W	124	89.9

The sampled population is approximately as diverse than our pool, but the 'n's are too small in breakdowns of ethnicity to find meaningful differences in the populations. All respondents started college in the Honors Program. 79.7% were Honors students in high school, and correspondently, 20.3% were not. All but two of the respondents from minority ethnicities were Honors students in high school.

Based on the collective experience of the authoring group, we expected that the primary draw for the Honors Program would be Priority Registration, with a potential second as the opportunity for a single room (about 95% of Honors students live in a single room). We also expected that the 15-hour per semester community service requirement might act as a deterrent to entry.

To our surprise, the "Leadership position" was the most intimidating requirement. In response to the question: "How important were the following in your decision to join the program?" 75.9% said Priority Registration was 'Most important' or 'Very Important" and 68.2% said the opportunity for a single room was 'Most important' or 'Very Important'. There was no meaningful difference in motivators or deterrents by ethnicity.

A substantial majority of current Honors students were Honors students in high school. The program could build relationships with Honors programs in minority-serving high schools in our geographic area. As we are not the flagship in our state,[9] we may have some trouble in recruiting, but recruiting small numbers is preferable to recruiting none.

---

[9] The University of Michigan has almost $60,000 annual scholarship (called 'HAIL') for high achievers "from rural and suburban schools, as well as urban schools, who demonstrate financial need and academic promise".
(http://www.insightintodiversity.com/michigan-to-expand-socioeconomic-diversity-with-full-tuition-scholarships/)

How does Honors collaborate?

Ferris does have two 'bridge' programs for students from underrepresented backgrounds: GEARUP and Promesa. GEARUP is run by the Office of Multicultural Student Services (OMSS). For those unfamiliar with the model, it is a seven-year program that starts no later than 7th grade, and continues through the 1st year of college. Our program reaches five area high schools: Baldwin, Big Rapids, Morley Stanwood, Muskegon, and Muskegon Heights High Schools. Three of the five: Baldwin, Muskegon High and Muskegon Heights High, are 'Red' on the state's rating system. Big Rapids and Morley Stanwood are 'Yellow.' It is probably little surprise to the readers of this article that the 'Red' schools are significantly more diverse than the 'yellow.' Muskegon Heights and Muskegon High are both minority-majority schools, with 97% African American at Muskegon Heights and 68% African-American at Muskegon. Baldwin (which is in the area of the historic African-American resort Idlewild) is 43% non-White. Big Rapids is 84% White, and Morley Stanwood is 95% White.

While the Honors Program anticipates greater collaboration with GEARUP in the future, we are not counting on it to diversify our pool significantly.

Promesa is a local summer program for Hispanic/Latino students from the Grand Rapids, Holland and Hart/Shelby areas started by our Center for Latin@ Studies (CLS). Honors has a longer history of collaboration with the CLS, meeting with Promesa students most summers to talk about the benefits of Honors and to encourage them to consider graduate and profession tracks in college. In fact, the two coordinators in 2014-2015 were Honors students, and the current director is a former Honors student. This relationship may be one of the reasons for the increase in the Hispanic / Latino population of Honors in recent years.[10]

Any Psychological Barriers?

A number of students suggested, informally, that there were certain psychological barriers to joining the Honors Program. Honors students have a reputation, certainly, and it is not always positive. Honors students are often seen as doing nothing but studying, antisocial in character, 'nerds'

---

[10] We do not have data about the baseline increase in the Hispanic / Latino population during this same period, so we are unable to tell if our increase is in proportion to the population growth or not. We will have to wait until the census of 2020 to make a meaningful comparison in this case.

(when that word is used in a derogatory way instead of a point of pride), etc. More importantly, some of the students from ethnically minority populations who were working on the project noted a number of implicit fears that should be considered. Students suspected a fear of not 'fitting in' with a program that is majority white, or not finding the support or connections they would need while existing in a program that was largely white. Those are to be expected, and will be addressed through better collaboration with Office of Multicultural Student Services (OMSS) and Center for Latin@ Studies (CLS).

They also noted their own personal struggle with being seen as a stereotype in the program—students of Asian descent, for example, report various interactions on campus where the opposite party just assumed that they were in Honors. They are, of course, in Honors, but resent the fact that that stereotype was applied. Second, there is a potential for 'imposter syndrome' for those from traditionally underrepresented groups.

It is this last point that we suspect explains the pattern we see in the admissions process above. If one has a tendency for imposter syndrome, every step in the admissions process is another point where one can talk oneself *out* of the process. A student plagued by self-doubt will, we suspect, see each request for confirmation as indication that the Program doesn't *really* want them. More research is needed, of course, to confirm or disconfirm this hypothesis, but we have begun the process of redesigning our Admissions procedure to minimize the steps required by the prospective student.

Anticipated improvements

Our final step in this was process was to review the results of our survey and determine any possible places for improvement. First, we believe it vital to better communicate the diversity that does exist in Honors, not just in terms of ethnicity, but also in terms of majors (not all Pre-Pharm, for example) and interests (yes, we have athletes as well!) to the community on and off-campus. Second, while we anticipate further collaboration with OMSS and CLS, we will also investigate Honors Societies at minority-majority high schools—relying on current students from those areas as ambassadors—and hopefully build our own pathways to Ferris complement and extend those constructed by OMSS and the CLS. Third, given our surprise regarding the concern of our leadership requirement, we must look carefully at that language and perhaps revise it to make it less intimidating for the prospective student. Finally, the students believe strongly that promoting the program as a developmental arc, rather than as an accomplishment or reward, would go a long way to convincing prospective students who do not currently consider themselves "Honors" to join the program. That view is consistent with the Director's philosophy of Honors, and the revisions we have made to our marketing materials since 2013. Finally, we have identified ways we can improve, and we will certainly make this a priority in coming years.

CHAPTER EIGHT

DISAGREEMENT, INCLUSIVITY, AND COMMUNITY IN (PUBLIC) HONORS EDUCATION

MATTHEW CAREY JORDAN

Introduction

This chapter takes a different approach than some of the other essays in this volume. Its goal is to offer a criterion for determining which sorts of views, if any, may be considered out-of-bounds in an honors community. This is an important issue for anyone seeking to maximize diversity and inclusiveness in their honors program or college, because the expression of certain views (e.g., racism, sexism, homophobia) at least appears to undermine the possibility of genuine respect for all members of the community, in which case these views may be appropriate objects of censure. Whether a particular viewpoint *does*, in fact, have this outcome is a more difficult question. Appearances can be deceiving, after all. We need a principled basis for setting the matter.

My methodology will be familiar to anyone with a background in philosophy. In the first section, I will lay out the problem: there is a tension in honors education that arises when we emphasize inclusivity along with critical thinking. In the second section, I will offer several cases for consideration. The point of these cases is to highlight the tension between inclusivity and critical thinking in ways that should be uncontroversial: I will take it for granted that the reader agrees with me about the proper response to each. I will then look at a number of possible explanations of why these responses are legitimate. I will argue that our overriding concern in all cases should be to establish policies that accord with the purpose of our honors communities, and I will conclude the essay with a brief application of that concept to the issue of gender identity.

For the sake of clarity, let me stipulate that everything below applies—or is intended to apply—to public institutions in a diverse, democratic republic. Much of it may be relevant to private schools and universities, and nearly all of it should apply to public institutions in pluralistic societies of other kinds, but whether and to what degree this is so is not something I will attempt to elucidate here. My focus is on issues of disagreement and inclusivity in publicly funded honors education, particularly (but not exclusively) in contemporary American institutions of higher education.

The problem

Honors education at all levels is marked by its emphasis on critical thinking. This is not to say that critical thinking is the only important feature of honors education, nor is it to say that only honors educators are interested in critical thinking. It is simply to say that, for all the differences in approaches to honors, it is unlikely that anyone has ever developed an honors curriculum in which cultivating students' ability to ask good questions, to consider and evaluate evidence, to make arguments, and to think for themselves is not a principal goal. Honors students are expected to exemplify the intellectual virtues traditionally associated with a liberal arts education: curiosity, open-mindedness, autonomy, and so on. Successful honors students are freethinkers, willing to engage with controversial issues and follow the evidence where it leads.

At the same time, educators and administrators who oversee honors curricula generally seek to create a maximally inclusive and diverse environment for their students. Again in the spirit of a traditional liberal arts education, everyone is welcome at the honors table. Students are invited to participate in an honors community without regard to race, gender, or creed. One rationale for this approach is that most of us take inclusiveness and diversity to be worthwhile in and of themselves. Inclusiveness, after all, is a way of demonstrating respect for others as fellow human beings, "free and equal in dignity and rights."[1] Emphasizing diversity does the same. In addition, an emphasis on diversity is an appropriate response to historical and ongoing patterns of structural injustice. But it should be noted that inclusiveness and diversity can also be justified instrumentally; they help us achieve our goal of cultivating

---

[1] UN General Assembly, "Universal Declaration of Human Rights," Article I (Paris, 1948), http://www.un.org/en/universal-declaration-human-rights/ (accessed December 21, 2016).

critical thinking skills. John Stuart Mill expressed the basic idea this way, in his defense of free speech:

> He who knows only his own side of the case knows little of that. His reasons may be good, and no one may have been able to refute them. But if he is equally unable to refute the reasons on the opposite side, if he does not so much as know what they are, he has no ground for preferring either opinion.[2]

When we create genuinely diverse and inclusive honors communities, we increase the number of perspectives represented within each community and thereby increase the likelihood that students will be exposed to "the reasons on the opposite side." Their views will be challenged, and opposing views will, one presumes, be vigorously defended. From the point of view of cultivating critical thinking skills, this is an ideal situation.

In practice, however, things are not always so easy. Some of the controversial issues that may come up for discussion in a classroom are intimately connected to students' own sense of personhood, their understandings of who they *are* on a very fundamental level. In our contemporary situation, some of the most pressing issues of this kind have to do with gender identity. With respect to such questions, how do we balance our commitment to free, open-minded inquiry with our commitment to inclusivity? On the one hand, questions about the nature of gender and its relationship to biological sex are genuinely complex. Answers to those questions are neither obvious nor uncontroversial. There are a host of competing views a person might hold. Thus this is precisely the kind of topic we ought to encourage our students to discuss and to think about carefully. On the other hand, the centrality of these issues in shaping many persons' self-understanding means that criticism or assertion of an idea—e.g., imagine a student who says, "I think that a biological male who identifies as a woman suffers from a psychological disorder"—may feel indistinguishable from an attack on a person: "you are mentally ill (and therefore your perspective doesn't matter)." What may appear from one perspective as a sincere attempt to engage with a theoretical controversy may appear from another perspective to be an attack on a peer.

The simplest way to resolve this tension would be to allow one kind of consideration always to override the other. That is, one could

---

[2] John Stuart Mill, *On Liberty and Other Writings*, ed. Stefan Collini (Cambridge: Cambridge University Press, 1989): 38.

maintain that the tension does not really exist: what honors education is about, at its very core, is free inquiry, and that means that every viewpoint merits equal consideration, regardless of its impact on other people. Or one could maintain that inclusivity takes pride of place: an honors classroom should be the epitome of a "safe space" on campus, where students know that their values and choices will be affirmed and that they need not fear being made uncomfortable.

Both of these alternatives are problematic. The former licenses too much; to say that every view is welcome is to say, among other things, that overtly racist and sexist attitudes cannot be dismissed as out of bounds. The latter may be even worse; in essence, it gives every student the right to shut down discussion whenever their own beliefs and values are challenged. So what do we do? How should we proceed? I believe that we can make progress by thinking carefully about three specific cases of disagreement, each of which involves an issue that is connected to individuals' sense of self in ways that may be similar to gender identity. These are cases (involving admissions decisions, classroom disagreements, and students living in community with one another) in which it seems a bit easier to make uncontroversial claims about resolving the tension between critical thinking and inclusivity. Through reflection on these cases, we can identify principles that are applicable to more challenging circumstances.

Three cases, four questions

The first easy case involves explicit racism. Let us imagine that a prospective student—call her Rachel—applies for admission to an honors program. She meets the program's admission requirements, has written a brilliant application essay, and comes across as charming and eloquent in a personal interview… until she mentions that she is a member of a white supremacist group. Rachel goes on to explain her sincere belief that fair-skinned Americans of European descent are genetically superior to all other races, and that our nation should work toward the goal of racial homogeneity. She is looking forward to starting a student chapter of the Ku Klux Klan when she arrives on campus.

The second case involves religious faith. Christopher and Anthony are students in the honors college at State U. They have both enrolled in an honors philosophy course focusing on religious questions. Christopher is an Evangelical Christian. He was born into an Evangelical family, has attended church every Sunday of his life, and cannot remember a time when he did not think of himself as a Christian. He has never seriously doubted the basic tenets of his faith. To the contrary, having been encouraged as a high school student to read works by popular Christian apologists, he is now convinced that the form of Christianity to which he adheres is objectively and uniquely true. He does his best to live out the teachings of his faith, and is considering a career in pastoral ministry. Anthony, in contrast, comes from a family of atheists. He has never believed in a god, nor has he ever felt tempted to do so. Anthony believes that atheism is not merely true, but that it is *known* to be true: his view is that an honest and intelligent inquirer should be able to discern that there is, in fact, no supernatural dimension to reality whatsoever. He also believes that religious faith, in any form, is harmful to the individuals who embrace it and to the societies in which they live.

Our third case concerns ethics. Valerie and Omar are suitemates in an honors living and learning community. Valerie recently became a vegetarian. She believes that eating meat is inherently immoral: animals, on her view, have the right not to be treated merely as objects, as things for us to use. It is wrong and unjust for cows, chickens, and other sentient beings to be held captive and then killed merely so that human beings can eat food they enjoy. She believes that the nature of this injustice is sufficiently serious that the consumption of meat should be illegal; criminal penalties should be enforced against anyone who knowingly eats an animal. Her suitemate Omar does not share her convictions. He loves beef, and routinely keeps steaks and hamburger meat in their refrigerator. He knows that Valerie is offended by this, and he enjoys pestering her about it, often waiting to prepare his meals until she is present and making jokes about the animals whose bodies he is consuming.

Honors educators and administrators need to decide how to think about situations like these. The four key questions raised by these three cases are as follows. First, should Rachel be admitted to the program in spite of her overtly racist views? Second, should Christopher and Anthony be told to enroll in a different course or, if they stick with Philosophy of Religion, to keep their opinions to themselves? Third, should Valerie's suitemates be required to share her commitment to vegetarianism? Fourth, should Omar be permitted to go out of his way to offend Valerie?[3]

I raise these questions not because I think they are difficult, but because I think that virtually everyone will agree that they are easy. The answers are, respectively: no, no, no, and no. It is appropriate to reject

---

[3] The language of "permission" here may seem draconian. I am taking it for granted that an honors LLC will include some kind of code of conduct, so the question here could be inelegantly framed as follows: *Should the code of conduct to which Valerie and Omar are expected to adhere permit the sort of taunting in which Omar routinely engages?*

Rachel's application. It is fine—desirable, even—for sincere Christians and committed atheists to engage with each other about religious questions. Valerie is not entitled to a meat-free refrigerator, and Omar is not entitled to taunt Valerie for her beliefs.

The genuinely difficult question is, why? If we may take the above assertions as a shared starting point, what is the principle that explains them? What makes it reasonable for us to say that some beliefs and attitudes are welcome, while others are not? Let us consider a few possibilities.

Agreement, offense, knowledge, and injustice: principles that don't work

One principle that would explain why we should answer "no" to the four questions raised above, and which might initially seem appealing, is the **cultural agreement principle**. This principle states that it is legitimate to restrict the expression of views within a community when there is broad cultural agreement about the issue in question. So, for instance, we might refuse to admit Rachel to our honors program because there is widespread cultural agreement that overt racism is beyond the pale. We can encourage Christopher and Anthony to engage in dialogue because we live at a time and place in history where many people are Christians and many people are atheists; both views are generally seen as live options for twenty-first century Americans. We will not insist that Omar's hamburger meat be kept elsewhere, because vegetarianism is a minority viewpoint in the broader culture. And since most people will agree that others' deeply-held convictions should be respected, we should expect Omar not to go out of his way to taunt Valerie for her vegetarianism.

The cultural agreement principle is not, however, a principle we should accept. There are at least two serious problems with it. First, defining the relevant "culture" is an exceedingly difficult—perhaps impossible—task. An individual may be a member of a large number of social groups, each of which may constitute a distinctive culture: one's professional colleagues may be characterized by a different set of attitudes than the members of one's hometown; a person may be a member of a religious group with a distinctive sensibility quite different from the nation in which she lives; a particular state or county might be out of step with the broader society; and so on. It is not clear *which* culture's values we would look to in order to establish the boundaries of legitimate discourse.

Second, and worse, the cultural agreement principle allows for a "tyranny of the majority" with respect to controversial issues. Once we have identified the salient culture, the people who constitute it could in principle shut down any opposing view simply by disagreeing with it. If we embrace the cultural agreement principle as our rationale for denying racists admission to our program, we would *ipso facto* be committed to tolerating racism in any community where racism is not viewed as being uncontroversially wrong. In other words: the cultural agreement principle would probably justify a contemporary honors program director's decision not to allow racists into her program. At the same time, however, it might justify a mid-twentieth century honors program director's decision not to allow egalitarians into his. Depending on how we define the relevant culture, it might even license a decision in some geographic areas today to deny admission to egalitarians. This is reason enough to reject it.

Another possibility is the **offense principle**. According to the offense principle, it is legitimate to restrict the expression of views within a community when one does so to prevent offending members of that community. Or, on a more refined version of the principle, it is legitimate to restrict the expression of views within a community when one does so to prevent members of that community from being *reasonably* offended. Either or both versions of this principle are sometimes appealed to in discussions of zoning laws, such as when a municipality wants to prohibit the opening of a strip club within its boundaries. For present purposes, however, neither version of the offense principle will do the work we need it to.

The fundamental problem with the simple version of the offense principle—in the context of an academic community—is that it makes it too easy for a group of students, or even an individual student, to squelch discussion of controversial issues. If we are serious about cultivating critical thinking skills, we need to be willing to be made uncomfortable; we need to run the risk that someone will express a view that is offensive to other members of the community. Christopher may be appalled by Anthony's disdain for the New Testament. Valerie may find it disgusting when others consume nonhuman animals. But these reactions, even if deeply held and sincere, cannot be allowed to stifle critical inquiry. The authorship, internal consistency, and interpretation of the Christian scriptures are legitimate topics of academic investigation, whether Christopher is comfortable with that or not. The nature of rights and whether it is plausible to ascribe them to nonhumans is an important topic in ethics, and Valerie's squeamishness about views distinct from her own cannot be the reason that her classmates (or she herself) do not discuss them.

The more sophisticated version of the offense principle, which stipulates that we need worry only about causing reasonable offense, is also not available to us.[4] One obvious problem concerns who, precisely, gets to decide what counts as being reasonably offended. What seems innocuous or even good to one group of people may be deeply offensive to another; consider, for example, contemporary debates about the nature of marriage or the legalization of prostitution. At a more basic level, we find essentially the same problem that affects the simpler version of the principle: in the context of pluralistic higher education, we cannot rule any issue or point of view out of bounds merely on the grounds that it is offensive, because such an approach runs the risk of eliminating virtually any nonmainstream, countercultural opinion from consideration. Perhaps there are some contexts in which it is appropriate for a group of people to do so. The public university is not one of them.

Here is another possibility. Granted that Rachel's overt racism is grounds for refusing her admission to the honors program, while Christianity, atheism, and vegetarianism would not be grounds for such refusal (nor are they views that should be suppressed), maybe the rationale is this: we are at a point in human history at which we now know that racism is wrong, but we do not know whether God exists or not, and we do not know whether vegetarianism is morally obligatory. Call this rationale the **knowledge principle**. The idea is that we could set the boundaries of legitimate discussion based on what we know to be true.

As with the offense principle, unfortunately, there are some fairly obvious problems with this approach. Setting aside the long list of epistemological disputes that would have to be settled in order for us to defend the key claim, it seems evident that—even if it is *true* that we now know racism to be wrong but do not (yet?) know whether meat-eating is, too—surely our reluctance to admit Rachel to the program is not due to a merely intellectual mistake we believe she has made. Consider: nearly all readers of this essay are likely to share my belief that mandatory vaccinations are an important part of promoting public health (and that we know this to be so), but, at the same time, few if any are likely to suggest that a student's professed disbelief in the efficacy of immunizations would be grounds for denying him admission to an undergraduate honors program. It would be rather bizarre for an educational (!) institution to maintain that capable students applying to a general academic program could be turned down for disbelieving or failing to know particular facts. It

---

[4] To be clear: whether the offense principle, in either form, is a plausible basis for zoning laws (*et cetera*) is another matter entirely.

is one thing for a medical school to reject applicants who do not know anything about biology; it would be quite another for a university-wide honors program to reject students for not knowing that vaccinations are highly effective. The mere fact that our belief in P counts as an instance of knowledge is not sufficient grounds for ruling assertions of not-P out-of-bounds.

What is more likely as an explanation of our willingness to deny admittance to an overtly racist student is a shared conviction that her attitude is not merely mistaken, but unjust. Let us therefore consider the **injustice principle**: it is legitimate to restrict the expression of views within a community when the views being suppressed are inherently unjust. This seems to be in the right ballpark, and would seem—at least at first glance—to line up with our intuitions about the four cases discussed above. It is not clear, however, that the requisite justice claims are suitable as policy guidelines at a public institution in a pluralistic society. The problem is that one of the key respects in which our society is pluralistic is that we do not have a universally agreed-upon understanding of what justice requires. A private institution may choose to govern itself in accordance with a libertarian view of justice, or a Rawlsian view, or a utilitarian view, or whatsoever view the members of that institution prefer. An institution that exists as a public entity in service of the public interest, however, does not have that luxury. To restrict the expression of views on the basis of a particular conception of justice is to favor one group of stakeholders' views over another's, thereby undermining its purpose as a public institution in a pluralistic society.[5]

Telos and the honors community[6]

Although none of these principles will suffice, the above considerations point us in a useful direction. If we can agree on what a particular university or academic program is *for*, we will be able to establish and evaluate its policies in a principled way: a policy will be justified when it contributes to the purpose of the institution, and will be unjustified when it

---

[5] Another option in this vein is to treat as "just" whatever the law allows, and to treat as "unjust" whatever the law forbids. The problem with this approach is essentially the same as the problem with the cultural agreement principle: it will sanction *whatever* the law happens to be.

[6] Some of the material in this section was influenced by Jonathan Haidt's talk, "Two Incompatible Sacred Values in American Universities," available online at http://heterodoxacademy.org/2016/10/21/one-telos-truth-or-social-justice/ (accessed December 28, 2016).

does not. Furthermore, we should be able to agree that the purpose of a public university is something along the lines of what was suggested just above: to serve the public interest. An honors program or college at a public institution will play a special role in helping the institution to fulfill its purpose, but that role cannot be one that conflicts with broader institutional goals. If State U exists to serve the public interest, then the State U Honors College does too.

Space precludes anything approaching a comprehensive discussion of what, precisely, it means for an institution or an honors program to "serve the public interest." Surely, however, there is nothing controversial about the following suggestion: *Honors programs and colleges at public institutions serve the public interest by forming communities of motivated, high-ability students, drawn from a diverse range of the institution's stakeholders, to pursue knowledge together in an intellectual forum and thereby become more effective citizens.* A particular honors program may supplement this purpose in sundry ways, but it is highly unlikely that any program would reject the idea that it is, at its core, an intellectual community whose alumni will be poised to contribute to the society in which they live. If that goal is indeed uncontroversial, then we have identified at least a partial purpose—a *telos*—of public honors education. And if we agree on a *telos*, we can establish and evaluate policies in its light.

Consider, then, the four scenarios with which we began. Rachel, the racist, may be denied admission to the honors program not because we have differing moral convictions, nor because her views are unjust, but because *her commitments make it impossible for her to participate in a community of the requisite kind.* This is the key. Overt racism of the sort she embraces denies that other students in the honors program have the right to be full-fledged members of the community. Christopher and Anthony, in contrast, may or may not become friends, but their disagreement is not the kind of disagreement that makes it impossible for them to participate as equals in the honors community. In fact, the opposite is true: each of them brings a perspective that enhances the community as a whole, understood in light of the *telos* above. Valerie's commitment to vegetarianism, and even her belief that meat-eating should be a criminal offense, does not conflict with the honors *telos*, but neither do Omar's omnivorous practices. Both of them, therefore, are entitled to eat as they see fit. Valerie is not, however, entitled to a meat-free refrigerator, because nothing about the honors *telos* entails a right not to be offended or not to be exposed to practices one believes to be morally wrong. At the same time, Omar is not entitled to taunt Valerie for her beliefs, because such taunting—as opposed to rebutting or critiquing—makes no contribution to the honors *telos* and, in fact, fails to demonstrate respect for Valerie as a peer; it is objectionable for a similar reason, if not to the same degree, as Rachel's racism.

What about gender identity?

The argument of this chapter has moved rather quickly, emphasizing breadth at the expense of depth. At the risk of compounding this error, let me close with a brief application of the core idea to the issue of gender identity. As was noted above, an understanding of one's own gender is frequently tied, in very deep ways, to one's sense of self; to who or what one is at the most fundamental level. The same is often true of ethnic and racial identities, and to individuals' religious and moral commitments. Some may object at this point and note that gender and race are intrinsic or unchosen in ways that religion and morality are not, and therefore that the former are essentially different from the latter, but this would be a mistake. It would be frankly ridiculous to say that a person like Christopher—whose personal history, friendships and romantic relationships, and career choices are all shaped in decisive ways by his religious beliefs—is free to choose some other set of beliefs and therefore his religion is not "really" central to his identity in a way that his gender is, or his race. Likewise for Valerie's dedication to animal rights and everything it entails. Even setting aside the enormous cost to Christopher and Valerie of abandoning their commitments, there are at least two reasons for treating those commitments as being as important to their identities as a trans man's gender may be to his.

First, there is the idea of integrity. Among the worst things human beings can do to others is compel them to act against their deepest convictions. Every tragic story of a prisoner who is forced to betray the nation he loves, or of a heretic who is tortured into professions of orthodoxy, bears witness to this fact. We can say the same about every hero who would rather die than renounce her faith or break a vow. If willingness to die for one's beliefs does not make those beliefs an essential component of a person's self-identity, then I confess that I have no idea what self-identity is or even could be.

Second, for all of the subtleties and complexities surrounding the issue of gender, one thing that cannot be denied is the strong sense of autonomy that makes the trans rights movement such a compelling cause. The spirit of that movement is expressed in the U. S. Supreme Court's famous statement, "At the heart of liberty is the right to define one's own concept of existence, of meaning, of the universe, and of the mystery of human life."[7] This understanding of liberty (and a commitment thereto) entails the right of individuals to explore and live out their gender identities in whatever way best suits them. *Mutatis mutandis*, the same right applies to individuals' religious and moral identities, and precludes a third party from privileging one form of self-identification over another.

These points are important because they connect the easy cases discussed earlier to more difficult cases concerning gender identity and various kinds of disagreement. I argued that racism may be treated differently from religious and moral convictions: we can (and should) tolerate disagreement about religious and moral issues without tolerating disagreement about the equality of all races. What about disagreement concerning the nature of gender? If a qualified applicant is committed to the belief that gender is binary, could that be grounds for denying them admission to an honors program? If someone is convinced that gender is determined by biological sex, should they have the freedom to defend that position in an honors sociology course on human sexuality? What expectations may we reasonably have for a traditionalist honors student who shares a suite with a trans woman?

Granted the *telos* of public honors programs and colleges suggested above, we are in a good position to answer these questions. Beliefs about the nature of gender are neither grounds for denying admission nor candidates for censure, because—unlike beliefs about race—they do not entail beliefs about others' ability to function as equals *vis-à-vis* the purpose of the program or college. The expression of those beliefs may be offensive or hurtful to some, but this means merely that the manner in which they are discussed is of crucial importance. In this way, they are akin to beliefs about religion and morality: controversial, important, but also legitimate topics of inquiry. At the same time, the respect that is required for peers to function in an honors community would entail as much mutual accommodation as possible; for instance, a transgender student may reasonably expect that classmates will employ the student's preferred pronouns, regardless of their own views on gender.

Obviously, much more could be said, and many more details could be explored. For now, let it suffice to emphasize that identification of a clear purpose for public honors education enables us to make principled decisions about what sorts of views may legitimately be considered out-of-bounds. Critical thinking, and the disagreements it is almost certain to entail, may come into tension with a commitment to

---

[77] *Planned Parenthood v. Casey*, 505 U.S. 851 (1992).

inclusivity. In a pluralistic society, in which there is substantive disagreement about a range of important issues, our best approach is one that mandates respect for each individual as well as open inquiry concerning every topic compatible with that respect.

CHAPTER NINE

UNDERSTANDING DIVERSITY IN HONORS IN A LARGE, PUBLIC, COMPREHENSIVE, HISPANIC AND PACIFIC ISLANDER SERVING UNIVERSITY: THE CASE OF CALIFORNIA STATE UNIVERSITY, FULLERTON[1,2]

SANDRA PÉREZ

To Bernice
En amistad y agradecimiento

Introduction

In spring 2015 when I applied to become the new director of the University Honors Program at California State University, Fullerton (CSUF), one of the priorities I presented during the interview process was to open the doors of our program so that more eligible students could benefit from the opportunities it afforded, namely priority registration and access to small General Education courses that run parallel to our mainstream course offerings. Our program requires a total of 24 units of Honors courses (at least 15 units of GE courses along with 4 units of colloquiums and 5 units of a senior honors project), including a creative or

[1] All graphs here included were created by Dr. John Gleaves, Associate Director of CSUF University Honors program. I am grateful to him for his careful work and for allowing me to here include the data.
[2] I am especially grateful to Dr. Allan Taing and Dr. Sunny Moon from the CSUF Office of Institutional Research for their support in gathering and sharing the data here included.

research-based senior project, and a total cumulative GPA of a at least 3.5 at the time of graduation. Without fully understanding the academic journeys of the almost 800 students enrolled in the CSUF University Honors Program in 2015-2016, I sought to maintain past administrative practices with the support of an Advisory Board. My goal was to give myself that initial year to better understand our community in order to make more meaningful adjustments beginning my second year leading the program. At the time, I had support from both the Provost and Associate Vice President for Academic Programs to grow the program in order for it to expand beyond the 2% of the student population who were enrolled. I believed (and still do) that the program's long-term goal should be to house the top 5% of the most talented and inquisitive students across all our colleges, mirroring the demographics of the university as a whole. In summer 2016 both top administrators moved to different institutions and the current situation has shifted.

Our Students

CSUF is one of the larger campuses that make up the California State University system with a total of 23 campuses. As a large, regional, public, comprehensive institution, CSUF serves mostly a local population of students whose families many times cannot afford the more expensive University of California campuses nor to pay living expenses for their children to move out of the home. Most students on our campus commute, have jobs, and juggle family responsibilities along with their studies. Our University Honors Program is a community of students, faculty and staff who within our large institution reaffirm our love to learn and foster opportunities for intellectual discussions and inquiry to ultimately flourish professionally and as human beings. As is the case at one of our neighboring CSU campuses, the President of Cal Poly Pomona in 2015 explained, "Honors students experience the best of both worlds, the enriching personalized experience of a small college and the numerous and varied opportunities only a large university can provide".[3] These benefits are available at CSUF where we were more recently better able to understand our students through data provided by our Office of Institutional Research; they provided the needed details on our past and currently enrolled students. Additionally, I have the support this academic

---

[3] Soraya M. Coley. "The Egalitarianism of Honors at a Polytechnic University." *Journal of the National Collegiate Honors Council* 162 (2015): 19-22.

Gender of Honors

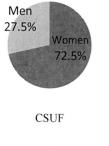

CSUF

Figure 1. Compares Gender of University Honors students vs. CSUF as a whole
Source: CSUF Office of Institutional Research and Dr. John Gleaves, Associate
Professor of Kinesiology, CSUF, January 2017.

year of my colleague and current Associate Director for the University
Honors Program, Dr. John Gleaves[3]. He worked with the data to create the
included graphs that were shared with both our Advisory Council and our
current Interim Associate Vice President for Academic Programs to try to
access more resources. Within our university, the University Honors
Program is mostly made up of women (72.5% Fall 2016). In relation to the
campus as a whole, we have 16.5% more women than men enrolled in our
program (see Figure 1). At 32.6% we are also overrepresented most in
students identifying as White (12% more than CSUF as a whole) and
greatly underrepresented in students identifying as Hispanic (we have 11%
less students who identify as Hispanic than CSUF as a whole). Our ethnic
breakdown Fall 2016 was 0% American Indian, 21% Asian / Pacific
Islander, 1% Black, 3% International, 6% Multi-race, and 5% Unknown
(see Figure 2). Although these are interesting percentages and in many
campuses would demonstrate significant diversity, in the context of CSUF
they point to a couple of deficiencies. We need to open our data to include
broader gender identity that allows students to self-identify beyond the
male/female binary as well as do a better job of recruiting our high
performing students who identify in the larger campus as Hispanic or Latino.

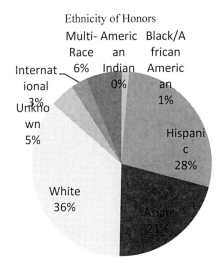

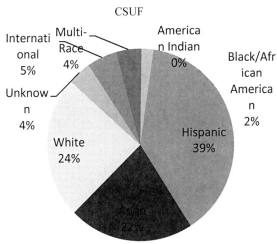

Figure 2. Shows ethnicity of University Honors students vs. CSUF as a whole
Source: CSUF Office of Institutional Research and Dr. John Gleaves, Associate Professor of Kinesiology, CSUF, January 2017.

As Víctor B. Sáenz points out in "The Latino Agenda is the National Agenda" from May 2016, "The latest census data, from July 1, 2014, show a population of 55.4-million Latinos. By 2060 that number is projected to more than double to about 119 million.

Of the 50-million students enrolled in public elementary through secondary schools in 2015, one in four is Latino and tlmost half of these students are in two states, California and Texas".[4] Thus, there is an especially urgent need in California for our recruitment to adjust in order to reflect greater gender and ethnic diversity in the CSUF University Honors Program. Based on 2014 data from the U.S. Department of Education, our university is number one in California and number four in the nation awarding baccalaureate degrees to Hispanic students. This placement carries with it the responsibility of offering all our students our best resources.

Our data also looked at the percentage of 1st generation college students both within University Honors and outside of the program. We are overrepresented with students whose parents graduated from college (23% more than CSUF as a whole) and we are underrepresented in students who are first generation in college (17% less than CSUF as a whole). This information underlines the need to make a greater effort to bring first-generation college students to our community. Our graduation rates are significantly higher than CSUF as a whole and they show that for every 50 additional students admitted into our program, we can improve the 4-year and 6-year graduation rate of the entire campus by .2%. Our community fosters a culture of success and opportunities such as a peer-mentoring program and a mandatory conference presentation for graduating seniors. In other words, the mere participation in University Honors ensures greater success in time to degree and prospects for any student enrolled. Lastly, our data form 2012-2016 shows that our Honors students can belong to any of our colleges who serve undergraduates. We are overrepresented in the College of the Arts, Natural Science and Mathematics, as well as Business. However, we are underrepresented in Engineering as well as Humanities and Social Sciences despite its significant inclusion in our General Education courses. Thus, our students are mostly females who identify as white and whose parents received a college degree.

---

[4] Víctor B. Saenz "The Latino Agenda Is the National Agenda." *Chronicle of Higher Education* 62, no.36, 2016.

1st Generation Students in Honors

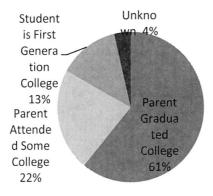

CSUF

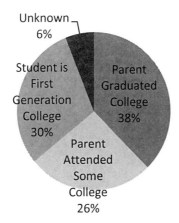

Figure 3. Shows percentage of 1st Generations University Honors students vs. CSUF as a whole
Source: CSUF Office of Institutional Research and Dr. John Gleaves, Associate Professor of Kinesiology, CSUF,
January 2017.

Current Situation

When I began as Director of the CSUF University Honors Program, I transitioned into a program that had been under the same director for a decade. There was pressure for change and I believe I was chosen in part for the ideas of growth and transformation that I shared during the interview process. In order for my envisioned transformation to occur however, we needed to create a new framework that would fit with the university as a whole and its governing process. The effort of my first year was thus focused on collaboratively writing a new University Policy Statement (UPS) for honors programs on our campus that would encompass the newer college-based Business Honors Program as well. We also needed to create Bylaws that would govern a new Advisory Council specifically dedicated to matters of the University Honors Program. My initial year much energy was spent working with a dedicated Advisory Board to put the two documents in place while the board simultaneously chose to dissolve itself and begin anew the following year. After many meetings and conversations with our Academic Senate, we finally succeeded at the last meeting of the 2015-2016 academic year in passing our new framework. A second crucial effort succeeded that same year: hiring an Associate Director to help lead the program. Dr. John Gleaves, Associate Professor of Kinesiology was hired and we shared many conversations over the spring and summer as we prepared to achieve the goals set for the following year. Lastly, in order to help me create a better sense of community with our students, I fostered an important partnership with Housing, the Residential Assistant (RA) of the Honors floor who is one of our students and student leaders who demonstrated leadership and initiative in relaunching our student group, HSAC. A particular student-leader who served on our Advisory Board was also instrumental in helping me to move forward. Therefore, I ended my first year as a new director with important headway in creating the needed administrative framework, gaining greater support through the Associate Director position, and collaborating with our student leaders.

Among our priorities for this year were the creation of a new 5 year Assessment Plan and study abroad opportunity for Honors students, which had never existed in the past. We needed to complete mandatory General Education Recertification of some of our courses and wanted to bring new full time faculty to the program who would help us bridge with all the colleges as we built new recruitment plans and sought collective resources. In these areas, diversity also played an important role. Our new Assessment Plan includes a Programmatic goal to recruit more diverse students and faculty in terms of disciplinary focus, ethnic background, and strengths. For the first time in the history of the University Honors Program, we have made it a priority to have disciplinary representation from all the colleges serving undergraduates on our Advisory Council and this has already proved a crucial asset. Through consultation with faculty from Biology, Illustration, Civil and Environmental Engineering along with Economics, Kinesiology, Liberal Studies, Spanish & Latin American Studies, as well as Tourism and Entertainment Studies, we have gained insight into the needs of our students from various colleges allowing us to ultimately better meet their needs. For example, there had been a tradition of holding colloquiums on Fridays when most art students take major classes; by shifting our colloquiums to Wednesday evenings or Thursday mornings we have solved the previous conflicts they faced. Ethnically our Council also has representation from the same diverse student groups that we represent and this creates healthy inclusive dialogue as we take on the improvement of different pieces of our program. Thus, the recruitment of more diverse faculty has proved essential in students seeing in our faculty the diversity we want to support.

Unfortunately, despite having data that shows that we can successfully graduate students faster than the university-wide rate, we have not been given the needed resource allocation to quickly move in this direction. With the Provost position unsettled, we have been on stand-by waiting for key administrators to allow the pursuit of the directions we seek in bringing greater diversity to honors and having our own goals serve the university as a whole. As a large, public, comprehensive institution, California State University, Fullerton is both a Hispanic Serving Institution and a Pacific Islander Serving Institution, it has almost 40,000 students currently enrolled, making it one of the largest public institutions serving Hispanic students in the United States. When I asked our Admissions and Records office to please provide me with a list of 1st and 2nd year students who based on GPA qualified for our program during January 2017, I received an unexpected list of approximately 1,400 students. Despite wanting to bring them all into the program, I must first secure access to the resources needed to provide them with honors courses, faculty mentors, and advisors. This is why despite our data showing the success of our program and the many students who qualify, I am not currently able to recruit them all. Strategic recruitment however is a priority as we respond to new student applications for Fall 2017. We sent out over 9,000 electronic invitations for qualified students to apply to our program and expect to receive about 700 requests. Our target Freshmen class will be approximately 130-140 students.

Our Plan to Address Issues of Diversity

Due to our current inability to significantly grow our program, we have to be as strategic as possible in creating a diverse program that is inclusive given the available resources. An initial request to do an internal recruitment in the spring to bring more students to honors was not possible. Yet since we are still able to maintain our new student recruitment efforts, we have taken several steps in trying to ensure we recruit qualified students from all backgrounds. This has been done through the adjustment of our application, the creation of a new admissions rubric, and internal outreach to key on-campus offices.

Our application is shared with Business Honors and we decided that we would change our essay questions in order to ask students not only about their intellectual interests but also, how they see themselves contributing to a diverse community of highly committed students. Beyond GPA, SAT scores, and advanced course work, our application requests that students share their awards and contributions as leaders, community members, young scholars, and employees. We understand the biases already documented with standardized testing shown for example by Santelices and Wilson in their 2010 article: "Unfair Treatment? The Case of Freedle, the SAT, and the Standardization Approach to Differential Item Functioning."[5] Thus if our goal is to prioritize access, then we must value academic and service recognitions as well as international experiences that go beyond standardized test scores. In this sense, our hope is that the new application will create a better method for students to demonstrate where they have contributed both within and outside of academics, as well as through their life experiences. I want to add that this was done while not lowering our GPA requirement. In fact, we raised it from a 3.5 to a 3.6 since the incoming Freshmen class to CSUF of 2015 had a mean GPA that was over the 3.5 mark.

Traditionally our recruitment plan has been to reach out to all eligible applicants who demonstrate high academic achievement and invite them to apply. Our Office of Admissions and Records provides the contacts for admitted students who are eligible for the University Honors Program. Candidates receive an invitation and then they can choose to apply. Under my leadership last year, there were no formal efforts to recruit underrepresented students. I did however, informally talk with colleagues in our EOP Office, advisors who offer scholarships to underrepresented

---

[5] María Verónica Santelices and Mark Wilson, "Unfair Treatment? The Case of Freedle, the SAT, and the Standardization Approach to Differential Item Functioning." *Harvard Educational Review* 80, no.1 (2010): 106-134.

students, representatives from our various cultural centers, and colleagues who advise students across campus. I also spoke at a local event for Latino male high school students in order to encourage them to continue their education, see the connection between higher education and potential access to better paying jobs that would in turn help them fulfill cultural expectations to be head of family financial providers. As Nadia Dreid explains in her article in the *Chronicle of Higher Education* on how the Metropolitan State University of Denver welcomed more Hispanic students through Stephen M. Jordan's leadership to change students' "life conditions and the conditions of their families" (A27). In other words, the goal cannot simply be to have the individual Hispanic student shine separately from their family or community but rather help them understand that such an opportunity will open resources for their community as a whole.[6]

Encouraging underrepresented students to, not only continue their education but to see themselves in privileged positions of leadership is crucial. Thus, as we continue to admit students, we need to make a greater effort to inform underrepresented students that the Honors Program is there to serve them and their communities as we encourage them to apply. For currently enrolled students, fostering internal communication has been beneficial as colleagues are inspiring more academically strong underrepresented students to apply. This year, we have made adjustments to our application in the hope that a new focus on how students contribute to a diverse community of scholars, broadens the background of our applicants. The message is that we value diversity and want to ensure it is seen as an asset for all students in our program. Through our new application for entering students this year, we want to continue to welcome for example, AP students who were very committed during their high school years, while ensuring that students who did not have access to advanced placement courses can also reap the benefits of being recognized. Our new application places greater value on contributions beyond GPA so that we can grow towards a more inclusive and diverse honors program. Through equity, we are making sure a maximum number of qualified students can access our program. This broader representation through diversity of background is an important contribution to our community; as students take on interdisciplinary dialogue and learning in their small seminar courses disparate views become a stimulating source for intellectual growth. This mindset is important to foster in future

---

[6] Nadia Dreid "Welcoming Hispanics." *Chronicle of Higher Education* 63, no. 8, 2016, 27.

generations of students: difference of background and world understanding are assets in trying to bridge people and communities. Understanding varying international perspectives, socio-economic and cultural backgrounds can only help us to deal with current global issues as our students transition into their professional lives. I am a strong supporter of study abroad but also believe much can be gained from embracing local diversity in global learning.

We have made this shift for our incoming students while continuing to accept applications from current and transfer students. We accept honors courses from community colleges and make adjustments where possible. It does become progressively more challenging to complete the University Honors Program requirements as students near graduation given that ours is a mostly GE-based honors program. Where possible, we do make accommodations through contract courses so students can meet honors unit requirements. Through these mechanisms broadening access for all students positively impacts the diversity the University Honors Program can achieve. Furthermore, as the president of West Virginia University explains in "Access, not Exclusion: Honors at a Public Institution", investing in the potential of all our local students is a strategic way to improve the region as a whole: "Honors students on campus make our entire university better, and having them in our community and in our state is an investment not just in these students but in ourselves".[7] There are various ways to enter the program either as a freshman or transfer student while support structures ensure greater success for all students involved in University Honors.

My Background

Given my desire to increase access for underrepresented students to the CSUF University Honors Programs, I do think it is important to point out that I myself am a first-generation college graduate Latina who excelled academically. I was not an honors student at the private, small liberal arts university where I completed my undergraduate degree but I was on full scholarship and was able to grow intellectually and mature from the experiences I was afforded at that institution. My doctorate in Hispanic Languages and Literatures then led me to be hired in the Department of Modern Languages and Literatures at CSUF. After my second year, I began coordinating the Latin American Studies Program and gained some

---

[7] Gordon E. Gee, "Access, Not Exclusion: Honors at a Public Institution." *Journal of the National Collegiate Honors Council* 16, no. 2, (2015): 180.

insights into administrative leadership on our campus. I have always been a strong advocate for students, especially those from underrepresented backgrounds because they have sought me out as a mentor and role model. I have tried to help these students gain the institutional understanding necessary to navigate higher education and succeed beyond graduation. My mentees have been from all backgrounds but they do include foster youth, undocumented students, underrepresented students seeking PhDs through the CSU Pre-Doctoral Program, student-mothers and untenured faculty-mothers needing to balance parenting responsibilities with their professional lives, study abroad students interested in Latin America, independent study students interested in interdisciplinary projects, as well as interns from various majors. My greatest contribution as a mentor and leader in these various roles has been offering flexibility in reaching desired goals. That flexibility has led to enriching experiences for me such as when I worked with five philosophy majors who were interested in Latin America. We met at a coffee shop on campus weekly to take on the study of Latin American philosophers through an independent study we shared as equals. We all contributed to the syllabus while collectively assigning reading and discussion topics to the group. It was wonderful!

In my current role, I see my mission as focused on expanding opportunities for eligible, underrepresented students while serving all students who naturally choose the University Honors Program. Thus, diversity through leadership is also important as I can bridge for current and future students the potential roadblocks in keeping them outside of our honors program. Furthermore, I hope to recruit more diverse faculty from more disciplines and ethnic backgrounds while also ensuring there is greater access for our students.

Conclusion

The issue of access is key for all students but especially for those who do not understand the opportunities they provide. On our campus, priority registration is a huge asset because it allows students to gain access to the courses they need on the first day registration is available each term. Honors students can carefully plan and actually get the courses they want. This opportunity also shortens the time to graduation. Furthermore, we offer enhanced learning opportunities that open professional doors and support the whole student. For example, we typically partner with our Student Health and Counseling Center to offer wellness workshops, we share resources offered by our Career Center or Advising Center for the Health Professions so students can gain additional resources in job seeking or resume-writing. We also offer personal academic advising to all our students which helps them navigate requirements. Through these connections, students have greater financial resources and the cultural capital needed to gain better prospects. The mere communication of resources broadens opportunities for our students. As students use additional advising resources through Honors, we are better able to guide their studies and help them successfully reach both academic and professional goals with greater success.

California State University, Fullerton as a Hispanic Serving Institution (HSI) and Pacific Islander Serving Institution (PSI) is already serving underrepresented students, thus we do not need to go outside of our current student population to find highly motivated, diverse students. We have here explained that due to our location and current demographics both the university as a whole and the University Honors Program are inherently diverse. We have on our campus already made innovative strides to better serve Hispanic students through the Enhancing Postbaccalaureate 0pportunities at CSUF for Hispanic Students (EPOCHS) program led by our Office of Graduate studies under the leadership of Dr. Katherine Powers. That program successfully increased the number of Latino students earning master's degrees. I was one of several faculty members who helped offer special orientation sessions, lead family workshops in Spanish, and supported students. The outcome of that program as documented by Sarita Brown and Deborah Santiago's "Latino Success Stories Can Help All Students" was a "57-percent increase in Latino master's-degree candidates since 2010 and nearly closed the gap in the graduation rate between Latino and white students".[8]

Likewise, the University Honors Program needs to better reflect the ethnic diversity of CSUF as a whole. We need to do a better job of recruiting more diverse students so that we serve our top students across colleges, disciplines, ethnic backgrounds, gender identity, and socio-economic status. To achieve this goal we do not need to lower admissions standards, rather we need to use different recruitment mechanisms that communicate a sense of belonging to our potential students. We have begun creating transformational support systems for all our students through broader disciplinary and ethnic representation from our faculty, a new assessment plan that values diversity, and expansion of contributing student assets through our new application. We do not currently have the means to offer our students additional financial assistance but our small

---

[8] Sarita Brown and Deborah Santiago. 2016. "Latino Success Stories Can Help All Students." *Chronicle of Higher Education* 63, no.9, 2016, 37.

classes, discussion-based learning, priority registration, extra attention from faculty teaching in our program, opportunity to lead a creative or research-based interdisciplinary senior honors project, demonstrated successful college experience along with completion of degrees, expanded professional opportunities, and additional mentoring are huge factors not only in offering greater opportunities to the students who most need them but also increasing their ability to transform their own communities thsrough greater access for themselves and their families.

Our main focus is to turn to our current and future student population to help them self-identify as honors and seek the benefits of participating in our inclusive learning community. By reaching out to students with less resources, we simultaneously address the issue of equity in education and better prepare underrepresented students to become advocates for themselves with greater social and cultural capital. Given our current data, we need to open avenues for Hispanic and 1st generation students in particular to self-select as honors students, to see that it is both financially and academically better for them to be in a learning environment that helps them reach graduation at a faster and more successful rate than if they remained on campus without our resources. We know that one of the current hurdles in growing our diverse student population is having students see themselves as belonging in an honors program. Therefore, our attention needs to remain focused on bringing qualified underrepresented students to honors. We need to continue recruiting first year students while inviting current students to apply. By offering students a more inclusive environment, a space to learn and grow as a community, resources to reach their professional goals, and the institutional knowledge to network across campus, we foster success for all students. Then as our services reach more students, we can improve the institutional graduation rates while truly serving all our populations of students including Hispanic and first generation college students. Honors students in general are curious in nature and want to go beyond their majors to explore professions or ideas beyond a traditional department's offerings, we can do this while supporting their goals and valuing diverse contributions within our community. The senior honors project offers this opportunity for intellectual exploration that can be more inclusive and meaningful to diverse community members.

Our new application seeks to minimize GPA, SAT scores, and weigh recommender's comments in relation to the limited space provided by the on-line application. It simultaneously seeks to highly value student contributions beyond academics in order to evaluate the whole student and his/her potential to be a contributing participant of our learning community.

Students have access through the CSUF University Honors Program to an affordable liberal arts type education at a large, public institution that necessitates all students participate as important contributors to learning and better global understanding. We have made some progress in creating the needed administrative framework that can help grow and support our program but we still need to open the doors to more students who can be formed in an inclusive, diverse, and civically engaged group in order to transform their own lives and communities.

CHAPTER TEN

MULTI-YEAR INITIATIVES FOR ENHANCING DIVERSE STUDENTS' OUTCOMES WITHIN LARGE PUBLIC HONORS COLLEGES AND PROGRAMS

DWAINE JENGELLEY AND JASON WARE

Introduction and Background

For at least 35 years, research on underrepresented minority students' academic achievement has suggested that this population of learners has achieved at varying levels and below that of their White and majority counterparts.[1] Scholars attribute this variance in educational attainment and academic achievement to several variables. These variables have been categorized as cultural limitations, moral deficits, intellectual inferiority, and oppositional dispositions. In this chapter, our discussion of these variables is restricted to the negative influence on high-achieving underrepresented minority students' self-efficacy within a mid-western honors college. We posit that the Honors College students within this mid-western university are generally high academic achievers. We will focus, then, on what we propose can be instrumental in enhancing their retention and post-graduate success. Throughout this chapter we will present a response to and an intervention for the social and academic effects of labels, and in some cases, real material differences, on students' matriculation. First we will define and discuss how we conceptualize a

---

[1] *see* Gloria Ladson-Billings, "From the achievement gap to the education debt: Understanding achievement in US schools." *Educational researcher* 35 (7), (2006), 3-12; Geneva Gay, "Teaching to and through cultural diversity." *Curriculum Inquiry* 43 (1), (2013), 48-70; Shawn A. Ginwright, *Black youth rising: Activism and radical healing in urban America*, Teachers College Press (2010).

tiered-mentor program and why we suggest it can be useful within a particular context. Then we will present briefly the student data used to inform the structure of the program. We will follow that brief discussion with details about the three tiers - peer, faculty, and alumni - of the mentor program. Then we will conclude by proposing ideas to assess the effectiveness of the program over time.

What is a Tiered-Mentor Program?

A tiered-mentorship program is one that exists to facilitate students' academic and social development as it relates to becoming a scholar, and is one that incorporates peer, faculty, and alumni mentors towards this end. It is designed to serve undergraduate students as they progress from tier to tier, from first-year to senior students, and because the mentors themselves represent tiers as peers, faculty, and alumni. The proposition is that students' academic and social needs change as they advance through their undergraduate education and enter either graduate school or industry. A tiered-mentorship program, then, functions to provide varying resources to students as their needs change and as they develop as scholars.

Why We're Proposing a Tiered-Mentor Program

Colleges and universities across the United States struggle to retain underrepresented minority (URM) students.[2] Retention problems are more pronounced at predominantly white institutions; although some of their recruitment initiatives increase the number of first-year URMs. As Rutgers University-New Brunswick welcomes more URMs on campus than they have in previous years, they also graduate about 12% more students of color than they did ten years ago.[3] This sort of twofold increase has not yet become common throughout predominantly white institutions, which is to say campuses like ours experience the opposite. What we find within our university is that we attract increased numbers of URM students, but have a difficult time keeping them on campus; they leave our institution to go to another. We posit that this challenge is exacerbated within the Honors

---

[2] RT Palmer, RJ Davis, DC Maramba, "Role of an HBCU in supporting academic success for underprepared Black Males", *Negro Educational Review,* (2010).
[3] Danielle Douglas-Gabrielle, "Similar colleges. Similar population of black students. So why the disparate graduation rates?" *The Washington Post,* https://www.washingtonpost.com/news/grade-point/wp/2016/03/23/similar-colleges-similar-population-of-black-students-so-why-the-disparate-graduation-rates/?utm_term=.9718c180a11e (2016)

College by our curricular requirements and our scholar development focus. We suggest this is the case because of the additional load, not for any reasons related to students' intellectual ability or propensity to persist. One implication of this challenge is a greater need for focused effort to retain and develop URM students. We argue that a tiered mentorship program can help mitigate the risk of losing URM students recruited to our University's Honors College because it can center students' social, academic, and postgraduate development.[4]

Many colleges and universities that attract large numbers of URM students, such as historically black colleges and universities (HBCU), foster academic success through community building and peer groups. Due in part to the racial homogeneity of the faculty and students, some HBCU students attribute their academic successes to the community formed by caring faculty and staff.[5] Students from these campuses have stated that seeing Black peers and faculty who have been and are academically successful encourages them that they can do the same. This kind of community of Black faculty, staff, and peers provides URM students with counter-narratives, opposing the dominant one which suggests they have cultural limitations, moral deficits, and that they are intellectually inferior to their White peers. The peer groups URM students form within HBCU have been known to "...influence their desire to perform well academically..." because their friends are "...serious and driven..." and happen to look like them.[6] On predominantly White campuses like ours, we lack this sort of racial homogeneity and consequently the community and peer groups that can accompany it. One primary tenet of the tiered mentor program we envision involves fostering peer, faculty, and alumni connections that create a comparable community.

Mentor programs are common among the many predominantly white institutions with honors programs and colleges in the United States. There are mentor programs for first-year students as they transition from high school to the college or university and into their honors programs/colleges specifically. There are less structured faculty mentorships that exist within undergraduate research initiatives, and we imagine informal faculty mentorships exist as a function of honors education. Campuses like the University of Maryland-Baltimore County have peer, faculty, and industry mentorships for STEM students. It is rare to find a

---

[4] Terrell Lamont Strayhorn, and Melvin Cleveland Terrell, "Mentoring and satisfaction with college for Black students." *Negro Educational Review* 58, no.1-2, (2007): 69-83.
[5] RT Palmer, RJ Davis, DC Maramba.
[6] RT Palmer, RJ Davis, DC Maramba.

tiered mentor program for URM honors students from varying majors, which is why we propose one. We posit that having peer, faculty, and alumni mentorships in concert will be more effective within our context than they are in isolation.

Student and Data-Informed Program Development

We contribute to the scholarship on undergraduate mentorship programs with original data collected from URM students enrolled in the Honors College. All URM students in the College were invited to participate in focus groups about their transition and experience in the Honors College with the purpose of developing URM student retention mechanisms. To supplement the focus groups, students also received an online survey that covered similar questions to those from the focus group. The response rate for the survey was 31 percent. Response rates for a survey of this kind is usually 15-20%,[7] and rates between 30 and 40 percent are considered enough for statistical confidence.

We used student input and data to inform the framework for the tiered-mentor program. We launched the planning and development phases of this project with a commitment to involve URM students throughout every phase of the creation, implementation, and assessment processes. Aware that multiple forms and types of mentor programs exist on our campus, we had no desire to duplicate their efforts or to add another series of checklists to our students' already heavy workloads. We decided, then, to obtain primary data from our Honors College URM students about the nature of their transition from high school to the University, and about the nature of their social and academic successes and challenges. Our methods involved focus-group interviews and a survey. We initiated data collection in the spring semester of 2016, and at that time 157 URM students were enrolled in the Honors College. Of the 157 students, 6 agreed to participate in focus group interviews, and 48 students responded to our survey. We selected two URM students from among one of our College's scholar groups to lead the focus group interviews and to inform our development of the survey questions. During the focus group interviews, the student researchers asked questions such as:

---

[7] Anol Bhattacherjee, *Social Science Research: Principles, Methods, and Practices*. Tampa: University of South Florida, 2012.

> ...tell me a little a bit about what your transition from high school into the Honors College was like...
>
> ...so what has been most helpful to your transition from high school...into the Honors College and into [our University]?
>
> ...what expectations do you have of the Honors College in terms of your personal development and growth?
>
> ...in what ways would having faculty and peer mentors further facilitate your success within the University and the Honors College?
>
> ...in creating a Honors College mentor program, it would have a peer aspect, a faculty aspect, and an alumni aspect. What is the value of each of those that you find in having like a peer mentor, or a faculty mentor, or an alumni mentor?

We distributed a 25-item survey that included 11 open-ended questions. Within the survey we asked respondents to use a Likert scale to indicate the degree to which they agreed with statements such as:

> My transition from high school to the Honors College was more challenging than I thought it would be.
>
> My transition from high school to the Honors College was challenging because I didn't have a sense of community when I arrived.
>
> Being able to connect with Honors College faculty helped smooth my transition from high school to the Honors College.

The open-ended questions invited respondents to share their thoughts about prompts such as:

> I need faculty to mentor me in the following ways and/or areas to help me be successful within the Honors College.
>
> Right now I am being mentored through the following programs.
>
> If I were to develop a mentor program for URM within the Honors College, it would contain the following elements.

Elements of the Tiered-Mentorship Program

Students' responses to both the focus group interviews and the survey provided meaningful data, which we used to inform the tiered structure of our mentor program. The program, as we conceptualize it, will include peer, faculty and alumni mentors, each level or tier providing unique resources to URM students within the Honors College. We describe the form and function of each tier in the subsequent sections. See figure 1.1.

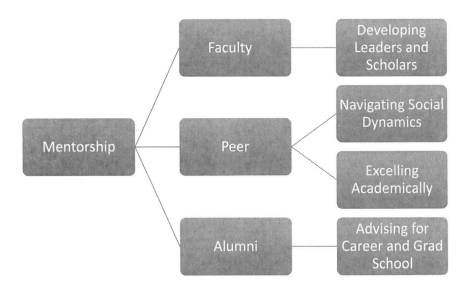

Fig. 1-1: Tiered-Mentorship Program

Peer Mentors

Peer mentorship is the first level of the three tiers we propose, which is central to a mentorship program designed for URM students. As undergraduate students who have recently transitioned from high school into the Honors College, peer mentors can share their campus experiences with first-year students to facilitate easier transition to the university.[8] Peer mentors are often role models because they have successfully transitioned into university life and are excelling; first-year students often see aspects of themselves in peer mentors.[9] Students are often more comfortable working with other students than they would be with faculty and alumni. The absence of a hierarchical power structure between peers facilitates an atmosphere in which uncomfortable issues are easier discussed. For these reasons, student mentors help retain URM students.[10]

We discuss two components of our peer mentor model, the first of which is navigating social dynamics. URM students that enroll in large universities are often academically equipped and compatible with non URM students, particularly high achieving Black students when compared to achieving white students.[11] Too often, though, there is a lack of general recognition that they belong in the environment.[12] Consequently, cultural isolation is a common barrier that URM students face, and are challenged to overcome.[13] Working through barriers of self-doubt related to internalized notions of inferiority only adds to the burden of high-

---

[8] *see* Angela M. Locks and Sandra R Gregerman, "Undergraduate research as an institutional retention strategy: The University of Michigan model." in *Creating Effective Undergraduate Research Programs in Science: The Transformation from Student to Scientist*, edited by Roman Myron Taraban and Richard Lawrence Blanton, 11-32. New York: Teachers College Press, 2008.

[9] Jerilee Grandy, "Persistence in science of high-ability minority students: Results of a longitudinal study." *The Journal of Higher Education* 69, no.6, (2009): 589-620.

[10] Sandra Gregerman, "Improving the Academic Success of Diverse Students through Undergraduate Research." *Council on Undergraduate Research Quarterly* December, (1999): 54-59.

[11] Sharon Fries-Britt, "High-Achieving Black Collegians." *About Campus* 7, no.3 (2002): 2-8.

[12] Claude M. Steele and Joshua Aronson. 1995. "Stereotype threat and the intellectual test performance of African Americans." *Journal of Personality and Social Psychology* 69, no.5, (1995):797-811.

[13] *see* Kathy Stolle-McAllister, Mariano R Sto Domingo, and Amy Carrillo, "The Meyerhoff way: How the Meyerhoff scholarship program helps black students succeed in the sciences*."* *Journal of Science Education and Technology* 20, no.1, (2011): 5-16; Steele, Claude M. 1997. "A threat in the air: How stereotypes shape intellectual identity and performance." *American psychologist* 52, no.6, (1997): 613-29; Reginald Wilson, "Barriers to minority success in college science, mathematics, and engineering programs." *In Access Denied: Race, Ethnicity, and the Scientific Enterprise*, edited by George Campbell Jr, Ronni Denes and Catherine Morrison, 193-206. New York: Oxford University Press, 2000.

achieving URM students.[14] On predominantly white campuses, most students do not look like their URM peers. This reality can be a problem for URM students if they come from racially homogeneous high schools. For some there is a stigma that they are student athletes, and were not admitted to the institution based on academic merit. Data from our survey suggests that students' experiences in the Honors College align well with this notion found in the literature. Of the students we surveyed, more than half (56%) think that their transition to the Honors College was more challenging than they anticipated. Thirty-five percent of them attributed their difficult transition to the Honors College to an insufficient number of students that look like them. In response to this challenge, some offered the following ideas for developing peer mentorship.

> I need peers to...relate with me and help define my path forward by sharing their experiences, so that the unknown and seemingly unmanageable will become less daunting.

> I need peers to...help me adjust to...social life more.

> I need peers...who have more experience doing what [I'm] doing explain the hows, whys, and wheretofors [sic] of it.

> I need peers...who can connect with me on multiple levels.

> I need peers...who are really engaged...to interact with...the social aspect is such a huge thing because academics...are kind of the main point...but having that social aspect is important.

We are designing the peer mentor tier of the program to respond to the articulated needs of our URM Honors College students. Incoming first-year students will have the opportunity to interact with recruited and self-selected URM upper-class peers (sophomores, juniors, and seniors) at informal social gatherings hosted to facilitate organic opportunities for them to get to know each other. Students' qualitative responses to our open-ended survey questions suggest this sort of opportunity for students to establish friendships that can grow into peer mentor relationships: "...every student is different and every student does college differently. Sometimes this interferes with peer mentor relationships because there's truly no right way...that's what making friends is for." Ideally, first-year

---

[14] Derek Hook, "Frantz Fanon, Steve Biko, 'Psychopolitics' and Critical Psychology" in *Critical Psychology,* edited by Derek Hook, 84-114. Landsdowne: Juta Academic Publishing, 2004.

students will be paired with a sophomore, junior, or senior peer whom will help them connect with other URM students throughout the College and University in addition to helping them navigate the social terrain in general.

Second, we discuss the importance of academic success. Excelling academically not only requires hard work, but it is deeply rooted in a social network that values and expects URM students to do well.[15] Students' narratives within the focus group interviews connect their perspectives to this notion: "...you're surrounded by people who know they want to succeed and know they want to go places. So the community is definitely one benefit..." Cultural isolation correlates with lower grade point averages and longer time spent in college before graduation.[16] It is critical, then, to ensure students are connected to well-balanced student networks and peers. When competent first-year URM students struggle academically, it is usually related to lack of support that is not always academically related (e.g., cultural support).[17] Their academic success improves when they are supported by mentorship programs.[18] A mentorship program that integrates URM students into the community with support from peer and faculty mentorship should help maintain students' strong performance.

Faculty Mentors

Developing leaders and scholars is one of the primary goals of the Honors College. All first-year students and some upper division students live in the Honors College and Residences, which is an academic residential community in which faculty work to advance student leadership and development based on a four-pillar framework. The four pillars are: 1) interdisciplinary academics, 2) leadership development, 3) undergraduate research, and 4) community and global experiences. The pillars provide a structure through which Honors College faculty and staff can frame learning environments that enhance students' critical and analytical

---

[15] Kathy Stolle-McAllister, Mariano R Sto Domingo, and Amy Carrillo. 2011. "The Meyerhoff way: How the Meyerhoff Scholarship Program Helps Black Students Succeed in the Sciences." *Journal of Science Education and Technology* 20, no.1 (2011): 5-16.

[16] Claude M. Steele and Joshua Aronson. 1995. "Stereotype threat and the intellectual test performance of African Americans." *Journal of Personality and Social Psychology* 69, no.5 (1995): 797-811.

[17] *see* Steele (1997), Wilson (2000).

[18] *see* Gregerman (1999), Strayhorn and Terrell (2007).

thinking skills, teamwork and collaboration skills, interdisciplinary problem solving skills, and general communication skills. This focus and design is for all Honors College students. However, the degree to which URM students have achieved these outcomes is still under investigation, because the Honors College is the newest academic college at the university, formed in 2013. What University data suggests on a broader level is that 83.5% of the 2013 cohort (4916 students) of incoming first-year students remained enrolled as of fall 2016, and that of the URM students (436), 77.2% were retained. We make sense of this data in part by acknowledging that the gap in retention between URM students and their non-URM peers demands our attention as the Honors College moves forward in developing leaders and scholars. We will have fewer students to develop if they are leaving campus *en masse*. Keeping rates of attrition low is a priority if we wish to facilitate a sustained four-year student development program based on the pillars of the Honors College. The role of the faculty in this process is even greater than advancing the pillars. Encouraging URM students to remain in the Honors College is equally about helping them understand the benefits of the college and showing them that they not only belong, but are important to the College. In fact, we suggest using the pillars to mentor URM students. Particularly, we emphasize a focus on developing student leaders through deliberate experiences and contact with faculty. Furthermore, we posit that integrating undergraduates in faculty research with a goal of treating students as partners in the discovery process and not as research assistants, can bolster student development, improve faculty student relationships, and create new knowledge.[19]

There is strong support from our students for faculty mentorship, as 80% of URM students believe having faculty mentors will assist them in being successful within the University. Just under 50 percent (44.74) of the URM students surveyed attribute a smoother transition to the college to faculty involvement and support. Below are a sample of sentiments students expressed supporting the need for faculty mentors.

> I need faculty to mentor me in...transitioning to college, professional development, academic success.

---

[19] James N. Druckman, "Merging Research and Undergraduate Teaching in Political Behavior Research." *PS: Political Science & Politics* 48, no.1 (2014): 53-57.

> I think it is sometimes unclear what is required of us in the Honors College. A faculty [mentor] can help guide us so that we can accomplish an Honors degree.

> I need faculty to mentor me in...overcoming stress, character development, academic success.

> ...it's great...the honors faculty are some of the most outgoing and extemporaneous people sometimes. Like Dr.xxx, I share a lot with him sometimes, and he always asks how my semester is going. Being able to have that confidant, having someone like that to talk to is really great...

Implementing a mentorship program should provide more benefit to students than informal mentoring from faculty.

Alumni Mentors

In this section, we discuss alumni participation in the tiered mentorship program. Incorporating Honors College alumni into the mentor program will benefit both students and the College's retention efforts. The success of alumni mentorship has been documented in a number of mentorship programs across various disciplines involving underrepresented groups, take for example, *The Holmes Scholars Network*.[20] Alumni connecting with students create a networking partnership in which alumni share knowledge and experiences with students'[21] Alumni mentorship adds a layer of support that faculty and peer mentors are unable to provide. Take, for instance, alumni industry experience. We hope that alumni mentors can influence students' understanding that the non-field specific skills that their Honors College experiences foster are valuable beyond academia. The alumni mentors can serve as individual data points, as it were, supporting the notion that analytical thinking, teamwork and collaboration, and interdisciplinary approaches to problem-solving, are relevant skills that transfer from the classroom into industry and graduate study. Since students often view alumni as people who have successfully navigated university life and are now productive members of society, graduates can help boost the confidence of current students to stay in the program.

---

[20] Sara Lamb, "The Holmes Scholars Network: A Networking Mentoring Program of the Holmes Partnership." *Peabody Journal of Education* 74, no.2, (1999): 150-162.

[21] Lamb (1999).

The survey data we collected on current URM honors students indicates a preference for mentors that share similar demographic characteristics. Students provided narratives like the following within the open-ended portion of the survey.

> [Alumni mentors] - It's definitely someone who can help you be...think about putting your career in perspective. Because they have been where you are now or somewhere similar...

> For underrepresented minorities in the Honors College, a mentor program that contains...opportunities for connections with other minority success figures...would be beneficial from my point of view...

> Shadowing opportunities to shadow someone of your ethnicity or some other minority but in your career field so you can see some representation to keep you motivated...

While pairing current students with alumni of the same sex and ethnicity makes for easier connection with mentees and mentors, the pool of potential URM mentors at PWIs like Purdue, is limited. The early stages of the program will rely heavily on non URM mentors, a scenario we do not see as problematic.

Assessing the Program

All parties involved in the mentor program have a perspective that is useful for reviewing the program. A variety of evaluation methods is the best approach to gauge the impact the program is having on URM students. A series of pre and post focus groups and surveys, during the fall and spring semesters with student participants can help identify areas of strength and weakness of the program. We would administer surveys containing questions similar to those we used to develop this program. Focus groups will help clarify survey results and broaden the scope of information gathered about the program. As students graduate from the program, we can have them reflect on program effectiveness from matriculation to graduation.

In addition to enrolled student evaluations, peer mentor feedback is useful for assessing strengths and weaknesses. Peer mentors are likely to have higher rates of interaction with mentees than faculty and alumni mentors. This increased interaction with students makes peer mentors a valuable resource to evaluate the program. Individual mentor reflections about the nature of their relationships with their mentees can qualitatively evaluate their impact. Peer mentors are also expected to evaluate changes in particular domains such as, mentee autonomy, relatedness, and self-perceived competence, as a means of evaluating their influence as mentors.[22]

It is also important to use both the experience of faculty mentors and alumni mentors to gauge their perception of the program. Faculty members are uniquely positioned to assess if students are approaching acceptable levels of attainment and achievement. In the case of the Honors College, faculty can gauge if students are meeting the College's requirements for student engagement. The alumni survey would help gauge alumni perceptions about their contribution to student development. Long term, exogenous measures like rates of graduation and engagement with the four pillars of the Honors College will be used as proxy measures of indicators of program success.

Conclusion

In this chapter we discussed a mentorship framework for URM honors students at large public institutions; a framework informed by insights from URM students enrolled in the Honors College at Purdue University. Our proposed tiered mentorship program focuses on improving students' social and academic outcomes, a process for enhancing URM students' retention. Working with peer, faculty and alumni mentors, students have opportunities to participate in enriching college experiences, such as undergraduate research, community and global engagement, leadership development, and interdisciplinary problem solving. Research suggests that the nature of this kind of student-to-faculty interaction enhances students' satisfaction and the likelihood they will have enhanced social and academic outcomes. Structured intentional interaction with URM students is vital if universities intend to retain and graduate this population of students. URM students are receptive to this form of interaction. Students' insights suggest that mentorship programs that most appeal to them incorporate opportunities for students to interact with peers, faculty, and alumni at varying times and for various reasons while obtaining a university degree. First-year students, for instance, look to second and third-year students to provide course-level and social guidance. Which is

---

[22] Edward L Deci and Richard M Ryan, "The 'what' and 'why' of Goal Pursuits: Human Needs and the Self-determination of Behavior." *Psychological Inquiry* 11, no.4, (2000): 227-268.

to say they look for peers to help them navigate the course selection process, and to help them think through their extra and co-curricular opportunities. Students look to faculty to help them navigate the research process—what does it mean to do research and how should one go about reaching out to faculty for research purposes. Alumni, per students' insights, can help them make meaningful connections between what they are learning in the classroom and the practical world of work via insights and internship opportunities.

We believe this approach to mentorship will yield positive outcomes in the way of student retention. Similar mentorship models would benefit from employing the tiered approach. We plan to assess the program's impact and effectiveness to provide evidence that supports this notion. Intentionally connecting students with their peers, faculty participating in student development beyond the classroom, and incorporating alumni mentorship allow for multiple touch points that will bolster students' academic and social outcomes.

REFERENCES

"2011 CIRP Freshman Survey, CIRP Construct Reports, First-time, Full-time Freshmen, John Brown University," (accessed December 1, 2016)

"JBU Facts 2016-17," John Brown University, accessed December 1, 2016, http://www.jbu.edu/about/facts/

"Scholars Programs at UMBC," http://undergraduate.umbc.edu/apply/scholars.php.

Adams, Maurianne, et. al., *Teaching for Diversity and Social Justice*, 3rd ed. New York: Routledge, 2016.

Ashton, William. A., "Honors needs diversity more than the diverse need honors." *Journal of the National Collegiate Honors Council*, vol. 10, no. 1, (2009): 67.

Balemian, Kara and Jing Feng. "First Generation Students: College Aspirations, Preparedness and Challenges". Presentation at College Board AP Annual Conference, Las Vegas, NV, (July 19, 2013). Accessed February 1, 2017. https://research.collegeboard.org/sites/default/files/publications/2013/8 /presentation-apac-2013-first-generation-college-aspirations-preparedness-challenges.pdf.

Baltimore City Public Schools, City Schools at a Glance, http://www.baltimorecityschools.org/about/by_the_numbers, accessed July 26 2017.

Belbin, R. Meredith, *Management Teams: Why They Succeed or Fail*, London: Heinemann, 1981.

Bhattacherjee, Anol, *Social Science Research: Principles, Methods, and Practices*. Tampa: University of South Florida, 2012.

Bowen W.G., and D. Bok, The Shape of the River: Long-Term Consequences of Considering Race in College and University Admissions, Princeton, NJ: Princeton University Press, 2000.

Brown, Sarita and Deborah Santiago, "Latino Success Stories Can Help All Students." *Chronicle of Higher Education* 63, no. 9, 2016.

Cahalan, Margaret and Laura Perna. *Indicators of Higher Education Equity in the United States: 45 Year Trend.* Washington, D.C: The Pell Institute, 2015 Revised Edition. http://www.pellinstitute.org/downloads/publications-Indicators_of _Higher_Education_Equity_in_the_US_45_Year_Trend_Report.pdf

Charles, Laurie, in "The Value of Honors Education", National Collegiate Honors Council,
    http://www.nchcguide.com/about-nchc/value-honors-education/.
Chen, Xianglei and Dennis Carrol. *First-Generation Students in Postsecondary Education: A Look at Their College Transcripts*, Washington, DC: U.S. Department of Education, National Center for Education Statistics, 2005.
Clarion University Fact Book: 2015-2016 Academic Year. Clarion, PA: Clarion University, 2016.
Coles, Ann. The Role of Mentoring in College Access and Success. Washington, DC: Policy Institute for Higher Education, (2011). Accessed February 1, 2017.
    http://www.ihep.org/research/publications/role-mentoring-college-access-and-success.
Coley, Soraya M. "The Egalitarianism of Honors at a Polytechnic University." *Journal of the National Collegiate Honors Council* 16, no.2, (2015): 19-22.
College Board, AP Capstone Overview,
    https://advancesinap.collegeboard.org/ap-capstone
Cook, R., "An Examination of Issues Affecting African American Students' Decisions to Enroll in Honors Programs or Honors Colleges at Predominantly White Postsecondary Institutions", Ph.D. diss., University of South Carolina, 1999.
Deci, Edward L, and Richard M Ryan, "The" what" and" why" of goal pursuits: Human needs and the self-determination of behavior." *Psychological inquiry* 11, no. 4, (2000): 227-268.
Does Diversity Make a Difference? Three Research Studies on Diversity in College Classrooms, Washington, D.C.: American Council on Education and American Association of University Professors, 2000.
Douglas-Gabrielle, Danielle, "Similar colleges. Similar population of black students. So why the disparate graduation rates?" The Washington Post, https://www.washingtonpost.com/news/grade-point/wp/2016/03/23/similar-colleges-similar-population-of-black-students-so-why-the-disparate-graduation-rates/?utm_term=.9718c180a11e , 2016.
Dreid, Nadia., "Welcoming Hispanics." *Chronicle of Higher Education* 63, no.8, 2016.
Druckman, James N., "Merging Research and Undergraduate Teaching in Political Behavior Research." *PS: Political Science & Politics* 48, no.1, (2014): 53-57.

Elevation Financial Group L.L.C. Last modified 2016. Accessed Feburary 1, 2017.
http://elevationfinancialgroup.com/

Engle, Jennifer. "Postsecondary Access and Success for First-Generation College Students." American Academic 3, https://pdfs.semanticscholar.org/e27f/6b423579e29231e22446c0b7777 d7b5946bf.pdf (2008).

Freedle, R., "Correcting the SAT's Ethnic and Social-Class Bias: A Method for Re-estimating SAT Scores," *Harvard Educational Review*, 73, no.1, (2003): 1–44.

Fries-Britt, Sharon, and Bridget Turner, "Uneven stories: Successful Black collegians at a Black and a White campus." *The Review of Higher Education* 25, no.3, (2002): 315-330.

Fries-Britt, Sharon, "High-Achieving Black Collegians," *About Campus* 7 no.3, (2002): 2-8.

Gee, Gordon E. "Access, Not Exclusion: Honors at a Public Institution." *Journal of the National Collegiate Honors Council* 16, no.2, (2015): 177-180.

Ginwright, Shawn A. *Black Youth Rising: Activism and Radical Healing in Urban America*: Teachers College Press, 2010.

Grandy, Jerilee, "Persistence in science of high-ability minority students: Results of a longitudinal study." *The Journal of Higher Education* 69, no.6, (1998): 589-620.

Gregerman, Sandra R, Jennifer S Lerner, William von Hippel, John Jonides, and Biren A. Nagda, "Undergraduate Student-faculty Research Partnerships Affect Student Retention." *The Review of Higher Education* 22, no.1, (1998): 55-72.

Gregerman, Sandra, "Improving the Academic Success of Diverse Students through Undergraduate Research." *Council on Undergraduate Research Quarterly,* (December 1999): 54-59.

Gurin, P., Dey, E., Hurtado, S., and Gurin, G. "Diversity and Higher Education: Theory and Impact on Educational Outcomes." *Harvard Educational Review* 72, no. 3, (2002): 330-366.

Harrison-Cook, R.R., An Examination of Issues Affecting African American Students' Decisions to Enroll in Honors Programs or Honors Colleges at Predominantly White Postsecondary Institutions, Unpublished Doctoral Dissertation, University of South Carolina, Columbia, 1999.

Hook, Derek., "Frantz Fanon, Steve Biko, 'psychopolitics' and critical psychology." In *Critical Psychology*, edited by Derek Hook, 84-114. Landsdowne: Juta Academic Publishing, 2004.

John Brown University Office of Institutional Effectiveness, "2013-2014 Diverse Learning Environments Survey," accessed December 1, 2016.

Jucovy, Linda. *The ABCs of School-Based Mentoring: Technical Assistance Packet* #1. Washington, DC: Department of Justice, Office of Juvenile Justice and Delinquency Prevention, 2008. Accessed February 1, 2017. https://eric.ed.gov/?id=ED449433

Ladson-Billings, Gloria, "From the achievement gap to the education debt: Understanding achievement in US schools." *Educational researcher* 35 no. 7, (2006): 3-12.

Lamb, Sara. "The Holmes Scholars Network: A Networking Mentoring Program of the Holmes Partnership." *Peabody Journal of Education* 74, no.2, (1999), 150-162.

Leidenfrost, Birgit, Barbara Strassnig, Marlene Schütz, Claus-Christian Carbon, and Alfred Schabmann. "The Impact of Peer Mentoring on Mentee Academic Performance: Is Any Mentoring Style Better than No Mentoring at All?" *International Journal of Teaching and Learning in Higher Education* 26, no.1, (2014). http://files.eric.ed.gov/fulltext/EJ1043041.pdf

Locks, Angela M, and Sandra R Gregerman, "Undergraduate research as an institutional retention strategy: The University of Michigan model." In *Creating effective undergraduate research programs in science: The transformation from student to scientist*, edited by Roman Myron Taraban and Richard Lawrence Blanton, 11-32. New York: Teachers College Press, 2008.

Longo Peter J., and John Falconer, "Diversity opportunities for higher education and honors programs: a view from Nebraska", *Journal of the National Collegiate Honors Council*. 4, no.1, (Spring-Summer, 2003): 53.

Maton, Kenneth I., Shauna A. Pollard, Tatiana V. McDougal Weise, and Freeman A. Hrabowski III, "The Meyerhoff Scholars Program: A Strengths-based, Institution-wide Approach to Increasing Diversity in Science, Technology, Engineering and Mathematics," *Mt. Sinai Journal of Medicine* 79, no. 5, (September 2012): 610-23.

Mill, John Stuart, *On Liberty and Other Writings*, ed. Stefan Collini, Cambridge: Cambridge University Press, 1989.

Milton, John, *Paradise Lost*, ed. David Scott Kastan (1667), Indianapolis: Hackett Publishing Company, 2005.

"Missionary Kids," John Brown University, accessed December 1, 2016, http://www.jbu.edu/admissions/international/mks/

Morgan, Paul, (Elevation Financial Group L.L.C.), interviewed by Martin Dupuis, The Burnett Honors College, UCF, Orlando, FL, February 1, 2017.
National Collegiate Honors Council, "Definition of Honors Education", https://www.nchchonors.org/uploaded/NCHC_FILES/PDFs/Definition -of-Honors-Education.pdf (2013)
Obama, Barack, https://www.youtube.com/watch?v=2KzGZyO_lSU (2016).
OECD, Ten Steps to Equity in Education, http://www.oecd.org/education/school/39989494.pdf
Pittman, A., "Diversity Issues and Honors Education." *The National Honors Report* 22, no. 2, (2001): 28-30.
Planned Parenthood v. Casey, 505 U.S. 851 (1992).
Raehsler, R. "Survey of Honors College and Program Leaders on the Minority Achievement Gap." *Working Paper 201602*, Clarion University Honors Program, 2016.
Raehsler, R., "An Empirical Analysis of Academic Achievement Among Minority Honors Program Students." *Working Paper 201501*, Clarion University Honors Program, 2015.
Raehsler, R., "Survey of Honors College and Program Leaders on the Minority Achievement Gap." *Working Paper 201602*, Clarion University Honors Program, 2016.
Reeves R. and D. Halikias, "Race Gaps in SAT Scores Highlight Inequality and Hinder Upward Mobility," *Brookings Papers on Social Mobility*, February 2017.
Richardson, Robin, *Race Equality and Education: A Practical Resource for the School Workforce*, London: Association of Teachers and Lecturers, 2005, 6.
Rockquemore, Kerry Ann, "Allies and Microaggressions," Inside Higher Education Online, accessed December 13, 2016, https://www.insidehighered.com/advice/2016/04/13/how-be-ally-someone-experiencing-microaggressions-essay.
Rusert, Britt, *Fugitive Science: Empiricism and Freedom in Early African American Culture*, New York: NYU Press, 2017.
Sáenz, Víctor B., "The Latino Agenda Is the National Agenda." *Chronicle of Higher Education* 62, no.36, 2016.
Santelices, María Verónica and Mark Wilson, "Unfair Treatment? The Case of Freedle, the SAT, and the Standardization Approach to Differential Item Functioning." *Harvard Educational Review* 80, no.1 (2010): 106-134.

Savage. H, R. Raehsler, and J. Fiedor, "An Empirical Analysis of Factors Affecting Honors Program Completion Rates." *Journal of the National Collegiate Honors Council* 15, no. 1, (2014): 115-128.

Schoem, David, et. al., "Intergroup Dialogue: Democracy at Work in Theory and Practice," in Intergroup Dialogue: Deliberative Democracy in *School, College, Community, and Workplace*, eds. David Schoem and Sylvia Hurtado, Ann Arbor: University of Michigan Press, 2001, 1-2.

Seymour, Elaine, *Talking about leaving: Why undergraduates leave the sciences*: Westview Press. Some of the material in this section was influenced by Jonathan Haidt's talk, "Two Incompatible Sacred Values in American Universities," (2000) available online at http://heterodoxacademy.org/2016/10/21/one-telos-truth-or-social-justice/ (accessed December 28, 2016).

Southern Education Foundation, *A New Majority: Low Income Students Now a Majority In the Nation's Public Schools*, January 2015.

Steele, Claude M, and Joshua Aronson, "Stereotype threat and the intellectual test performance of African Americans." *Journal of Personality and Social Psychology* 69 5, 1995, 797-811.

Steele, Claude M. 1997. "A threat in the air: How stereotypes shape intellectual identity and performance." *American Psychologist* 52 6, 1997, 613-29.

Stolle-McAllister, Kathy, Mariano R Sto Domingo, and Amy Carrillo, "The Meyerhoff way: How the Meyerhoff scholarship program helps black students succeed in the sciences." *Journal of Science education and technology* 20, no.1 (2011): 5-16.

Strayhorn, Terrell Lamont, and Melvin Cleveland Terrell. 2007. "Mentoring and satisfaction with college for Black students." *Negro Educational Review* 58, no.1-2, (2007): 69-83.

Tutu, Desmond, https://www.youtube.com/watch?v=0wZtfqZ271w , 2013

Tym, Carmen, Robin McMillion, Sandra Barone, and Jeff Webster. *First-Generation College Students: A Literature Review. Round Rock: Texas Guaranteed Student Loan Corporation*, 2004. Accessed February 1, 2017. http://files.eric.ed.gov/fulltext/ED542505.pdf

UMBC Institutional Research, Analysis and Decision Support, Retention and Graduation Rates, http://oir.umbc.edu/university-data/retention-graduate-rates/.

UN General Assembly, "Universal Declaration of Human Rights," Article I (Paris, 1948), http://www.un.org/en/universal-declaration-human-rights/ (accessed December 21, 2016).

Wilson, Reginald, "Barriers to minority success in college science, mathematics, and engineering programs." In *Access denied: Race, ethnicity, and the scientific enterprise*, edited by George Campbell Jr, Ronni Denes and Catherine Morrison, 193-206. New York: Oxford University Press, 2000.

Wollstonecraft, Mary, *A Vindication of the Rights of Woman*, 2nd ed. (1792); Mineola, NY: Dover Publications, 1996.

Zúñiga, Ximena, et. al., "Intergroup Dialogues: An Educational Model for Cultivating Engagement Across Differences," *Equity and Excellence in Education* 35, no. 1, (2002): 7.

CONTRIBUTORS

Chapter One. **Simon Stacey** is the Director of the Honors College at University of Maryland Baltimore County and **Jodi Kelber-Kaye** is the Associate Director of the Honors College. Simon is a political theorist who received his Ph.D. in Politics from Princeton University. Originally from South Africa, he researches issues of global transitional justice and holds an affiliate faculty position in the Political Science department. Jodi was a faculty member in Gender and Women's Studies before coming to the Honors College, and continues to do research in the field, particularly in the areas of social movements and social justice. She received her Ph.D. in Comparative Cultural and Literary Studies from the University of Arizona.

Chapter Two. Dr. **Trisha Posey** is Director of the Honors Scholars Program and Associate Professor of History at John Brown University. A historian of nineteenth-century American religion and reform, her work has been published in The Pennsylvania Magazine of History and Biography, The Massachusetts Historical Review, and The Christian Scholar's Review.

Chapter Three. **Laura Hanna** is the lead advisor Valdosta State University's Honors College, where she also teaches interdisciplinary courses. Laura received her MA in English from Auburn University in spring 2015, where she also taught freshman composition and American literature. Fall 2017 will mark the beginning of Laura's fifth year teaching at the post-secondary level. As a doctoral candidate in education at Valdosta State University, Laura is writing her dissertation, which focuses on strategies to recruit more minorities to join honors colleges in the Southern United States. Laura's research interests also include approaches for intersectional inclusiveness in the classroom.

Chapter Four. **Graeme Harper** is Dean of The Honors College at Oakland University, Michigan, and founder of the National Society for Minorities in Honors (NSFMIH). He holds doctorates from the University of East Anglia and the University of Technology, Sydney. Other books include *The Japanese Cook* (2017), *Filmurbia: Cinema and the Suburbs* (2017), with D.Forrest and J.Rayner, *The Future for Creative Writing* (2014) and

Making Up (2013). He edits *New Writing: the International Journal for the Practice and Theory of Creative Writing* and *The Creative Industries Journal*, and is co-editor of the *Journal of European Popular Culture* and *Studies in European Cinema*.

Chapter Five. **Martin Dupuis** is the associate dean of The Burnett Honors College (TBHC) and associate professor of Political Science at the University of Central Florida. **Vanessa McRae** is the former director of the Office of Research and Community Engagement at TBHC. She is also a councilor and chair of the Diversity and Inclusion Task Force for the National Council of Undergraduate Research. **Zholey Martinez** is the program coordinator for TBHC's Office of Research and Community Engagement. She was also the founding coordinator of the Elevation Scholars Peer Mentor Program.

Chapter Six. **Rod D. Raehsler** currently serves as the Director of the Honors Program at Clarion University; a position he has held since 2013. Prior to serving the Honors Program he was the Chairperson for the Department of Economics for thirteen years and has been a faculty member at Clarion University since 1991. He earned his Ph.D. in Economics from the University of Iowa in 1993 and has published articles in econometric forecasting, economic history, economic education, and labor economics.

Chapter Seven. **Peter Bradley** is the Director of the Honors Program at Ferris State University. Once a systems administrator, his academic training is in Philosophy. He finds these two disciplines very useful in navigating the administration of higher education. **Jordan Dawkins** is a leader in the Ferris Honors community, having held a number of positions in the Honors student organizations. She is a fourth year student majoring in Accountancy Finance. **Melanie Trinh** is an Alumna of Honors and former Desk Service Manager for one of the Honors residence halls. She is now a P3 in the College of Pharmacy. In addition to being the new President of the Honors Student Council, **Cindy Tran** is serving her second year as President of the Asian Student Organization and her first year as Vice President of the Pre-Med Club. She is also an active member in the Student Alumni Gold Club and has been an Honors Peer Mentor for the past two years. **Caitlyn Toering** is a third year Honors student in the Dental Hygiene and Medical Imaging program.

Chapter Eight. **Matthew Carey Jordan** is the director of the University Honors Program and an associate professor of philosophy at Auburn University at Montgomery. He earned his Ph.D. in philosophy at The Ohio State University (2009), where he wrote a dissertation on theism, atheism, and the nature of morality. He has published several articles on this topic, as well as on pluralism and social controversies. When he is not thinking about honors education, Dr. Jordan can often be found cooking, cheering for Cleveland (Ohio) sports teams, participating in community theater, or spending time with his wife, Jen, and their seven children.

Chapter Nine. Dr. **Sandra Pérez** received her PhD from UCLA. She is professor of Spanish and Latin American Studies at California State University (CSU), Fullerton where she is also currently Director of the University Honors Program. She is president of the CSU World Languages Council. She specializes in Latin American narrative and has published articles dedicated to both modern and colonial Hispanic authors. Her articles have appeared in prestigious journals such as Hispania, Latin American Theatre Review, Alba de América, and others. She co-edited with Enric Mallorquí-Ruscalleda La Kloakada: Neovanguardia latinoamericana de los 80. She has participated in numerous national and international conferences.

Chapter Ten. **Dwaine Jengelley** is Clinical Assistant Professor in the Honors College at Purdue University, West Lafayette IN, USA. His research focuses on communication in matters of international security. Currently, he examines if the negativity in terrorism news coverage is influenced by the economic fortunes of media organizations. **Jason Ware** is a Clinical Assistant Professor in Purdue University's Honors College—1101 Third Street, West Lafayette IN, 47906. He centers community well-being in his research, and investigates the impact and educational effect of developing quality-of-life indicators with communities at the neighborhood and institutional level. Jason's research also includes exploring the effect of undergraduate research on students' ability to think analytically as well as their propensity to address problems from varying disciplinary perspectives.

INDEX